Good News for Young Athletes

GOOD NEWS
FOR
YOUNG
ATHLETES

Winning Strategies for Sports and Life

LAURA AND JOHN MOULDER

GOOD NEWS FOR YOUNG ATHLETES
WINNING STRATEGIES FOR SPORTS AND LIFE

iUniverse books may be ordered through booksellers or by contacting:

iUniverse
1663 Liberty Drive
Bloomington, IN 47403
www.iuniverse.com
1-800-Authors (1-800-288-4677)

ISBN: 978-1-4917-6118-2 (sc)
ISBN: 978-1-4917-6117-5 (e)

Library of Congress Control Number: 2015904880

Print information available on the last page.
iUniverse rev. date: 05/27/2015

To our children,
Brianne, Jack, and Aidan.
We love you!

Contents

Preface

The philosophy found in these pages is a blend of real-life experiences and the power of the Holy Spirit. As parents, we discovered that once our children stepped into the world of youth sports, we became armchair psychologists managing a wide array of emotions. The issues associated with the inevitable ups and downs of competition are varied and complex. Everything from interacting with teammates and coaches to dealing with skill level and achievement goals can be challenging.

While we provided encouragement, consolation, perspective, and advice, over time our children began to view this guidance as "what parents are supposed to say." The impact of our words diminished. Listening to other parents share similar experiences reinforced our belief that we needed to find a deeper well from which to draw wisdom. Our search led to an invaluable resource—the Bible. With a fresh look (and a little poetic license) at the intrinsic truths in this holy book, we developed a simple sports philosophy that uses a solid foundation of faith to achieve improved performance and a positive attitude in sports and life. We have seen the results of this approach with our children and would like to share this good news with the young athletes in your life.

Acknowledgments

As we go to print on this guidebook—almost three years after beginning the project—we realize that all good things are born over time. This book required the nurturing touch of many special people and the vision-enhancing process of, well, thirty-six months. And still, like all of us, it is a work in progress, awaiting the eyes and interpretation of its readers to truly bring it to life.

First, we thank God, who is all-knowing and all good. Through His spirit we were moved to take a deeper look at the intersection of faith and sports and realized that it can truly be a foundation on which our children build their lives both on and off the field.

We thank our children, Brianne, Jack, and Aidan, who made us parents and invited us into this topsy-turvy world of youth sports. They participated in many a roundtable dinner discussion about spirituality in sports and offered their own unique insights, providing the all-important youth perspective. They can be tough critics but really helped us hone our focus and develop a message in the vernacular of kids today. They have also been willing participants in our God-centered approach to youth sports, and as the saying goes, "the proof is in the pudding."

Brad King has been a tremendous resource to us regarding content, editing, and publishing matters. He spent countless hours reviewing our manuscript and providing valuable input, which helped us enhance the quality of this guidebook.

We appreciate the thoughtful insights of Robin Moulder, whose comments from the parent perspective enabled us to fine-tune areas of the manuscript to meet the needs of this key audience.

By sharing her own experiences in bringing a concept to life, Lee Anne McClymont encouraged us to believe in our message and offered important food for thought as we began this journey.

Thanks to John and Nancy King for their time in reading and offering an honest assessment of one of the first drafts of our manuscript, which led to some effective additions to the final product.

Pastor Tim Kuhn, of Faith At Newtown Church, and Father Luke Suarez, chaplain at Notre Dame High School in Fairfield, Connecticut, provided critical feedback specific to our Bible references and were also learned, spirited cheerleaders of our ultimate message. Indeed, they helped us lay the foundation of this guidebook.

Zachary Bokuniewicz listened to our ideas and created the graphics that brought them to light. We are most grateful for his patience, creativity, and willingness to go back to the drawing board to help us achieve our ultimate vision.

With deep gratitude to our parents, in-laws, siblings, nieces and nephews, aunts and uncles, cousins, and friends (and anyone we neglected to name who offered key input—sorry!) who listened, encouraged, and prayed for us during this journey and throughout our lives as well. We love you all!

Introduction

It's the bottom of the last inning. The home team is down by one run. There are two outs with runners on second and third base. A solid hit scores both runs and brings with it the coveted league championship. Your child digs his or her cleats into the dirt around home plate and stares out at the pitcher's mound. Suddenly the ball is on its way. The pitch looks good, and your child swings the bat. The crowd holds its collective breath ...

Welcome to the world of youth sports. While the action may not always involve such a thrilling finish, young athletes can expect many exciting experiences, valuable lessons, and other benefits through participation in sports. The physical activity is a healthy alternative to television and video games. They learn how to listen and take direction from coaches, develop interpersonal skills by being part of a team, and discover the importance of managing emotions through great victories and heartbreaking losses. They also begin to challenge themselves and set goals. Yes, participation in youth sports can be extremely rewarding on many levels.

Unfortunately, in some cases youth sports can become a breeding ground for overhyped travel teams, scholarship-obsessed parents, excessively intense coaches, ego-feeding personal trainers, and many other people who don't always have a child's best interests at heart. These kinds of influences can rob children of the character-building opportunities that come from athletic competition. Sadly, in some circumstances it is not enough to play for the sheer love of a game. Despite our best intentions, some children can get swept up into this unhealthy environment full of self-interest, false promises, and misguided values.

Whether your child is facing one of these challenging situations or you simply want to take his or her game—and life—to the next level, a faith-based approach promises the best and most lasting results. Start with the simple truth that God is within every person; in effect, He is our rock. We read in Psalm 18:30–31 (NIV), "As for God, His way is perfect; the word of the Lord is flawless. He is a shield for all who take refuge in Him. For who is God besides the Lord? And who is the rock except our God?" He is the solid foundation on which our children build their character, hone their talents, and navigate all victories and defeats. Once this wondrous gift is acknowledged, it can be tapped at any time and become a source of immeasurable blessings. This is not a passive, symbol-centered philosophy in which token gestures of faith will bring success or contentment. No, it requires active participation in the form of a personal commitment to physical training, Bible study, prayer, behavior modification, and nurturing a close, personal relationship with God though His son, Jesus Christ. To be clear, the intent of this approach is not to elevate sports to a higher purpose than it deserves. Rather it is an opportunity to meet young athletes where they are and to introduce them to the good news that will lead to an everlasting life of peace and joy.

Just as in every aspect of our lives, God's involvement in sports can seem a mystery. *Why didn't I make that team after practicing so hard? Why didn't we win the game when I prayed so hard for victory? Why did that injury end my promising future in sports?* The answers are known to God alone. His omniscience is beyond our comprehension. We are told in Psalm 139 (NIV), "All the days ordained for me were written in your book before one of them came to be." Those are some powerful words. God knew before Johnny was even born that he would strike out three times in a game when he was ten years old. He knew that Becky was going to make the winning basket in her high school championship game before she ever picked up a basketball. Helping our children trust in the power and goodness of God, while accepting His will for their lives, should be the cornerstone of any athletic training program. As the Old Testament promises, "Those who hope in the Lord ... will soar on wings like eagles ... run and not grow weary" (Isaiah 40:31 NIV).

Once our children acknowledge the role of God in their lives, it is much easier for them to maintain perspective about winning and losing, talent level, pride, humility, envy, and so many other issues they will encounter in the world of sports. They will avoid the emotional roller coaster of feeling superior after a great performance and inadequate after a poor showing. Accepting their individual abilities, performing their best, and embracing their role on a team become much easier when they recognize that God has a unique plan for every young athlete. Our expectations and those of our children should be tempered by this truth. "Lord ... All we have accomplished is really from you" (Isaiah 26:12 NLT). God is the driving force, not a coach, parent, or trainer.

God blesses His children with unique talents, but these gifts can only be revealed, nurtured, and truly enjoyed through a close relationship with Him and a desire to fulfill His will in their lives. Our children become athletes for many reasons, such as carrying on family traditions, trying to please a parent, wanting to be popular, or, as we hope in most cases, because they love a particular sport. When competing, however, their true purpose should be to glorify God, their creator. The apostle Paul states in Colossians 3:23–24 (NAS), "Whatever you do, do your work heartily, as for the Lord rather than for men ... it is the Lord Christ whom you serve." Our children don't need to prove anything to their parents, friends, or coaches. They don't even need to put pressure on themselves to perform at unreasonable levels. Ultimately, they are playing for God, using the talents He provided.

"By the grace of God, I am what I am" (1 Corinthians 15:10 ESV). This is the underlying principle and theme of this guidebook. When fully accepted and lived, it will illuminate the way our children live their lives. If God put the love of sports in our children's young hearts, we can assume that He rejoices when they display that love through athletic competition. No matter the level of performance or ultimate success, if our children acknowledge that their talents come from God and that they need only please God, they will be happy, well-adjusted athletes.

Although it may seem daunting at first, this can be accomplished when parents and children work together to discover their inner rock and identify the unique talents God has given them and how they should be used. The following pages are filled with reflections, suggestions, and applications for bringing youth sports to a new light in the hearts of our children.

This guidebook is designed to be flexible, with each topic a self-contained lesson. You may choose to read it from cover to cover or jump to a particular section of interest. It is divided into three main sections: The first, "Tap the Rock," includes six areas of study that are essential to becoming an enlightened athlete. The second section, "Embrace the Rock," highlights five of the most common issues children face in the world of youth sports and offers practical ways to apply the concepts learned in section one. The third and final section, "Treasure the Rock," reinforces the results that can be achieved by adopting this approach to youth sports. The topics covered and insights offered will provide parents discussion points to share with their children.

At the end of each subsection, there are four additional elements that will help children further explore the given subject. "Ripples from the Rock" are reality-based stories that give tangible examples of enlightened athletes using the concepts found in that section. Depending on a child's age, he or she may enjoy reading these and then sharing his or her reactions to the characters and themes. Following these engaging stories is "Start the Conversation," a suggested prayer to help children begin a conversation with God. "More Good News" offers a Bible story that relates directly to the topic at hand. Together with the many Bible verses cited throughout each section, these stories provide a wonderful way for children to start their own exploration of this holy book. Finally, "First Step" suggests an activity that will encourage children to take positive steps toward putting the lesson into practice.

We hope this guidebook will give parents and children an introduction to the greatest coach they will ever know—God—and a clearer understanding of His divine plan for them, both on and off the field.

Section I

Tap the Rock

The purpose of this section is to show our children how to tap into their inner rock—that is, to get in touch with God. They accomplish this by understanding what God expects of them, acknowledging the power of prayer, and practicing the virtue of godly living. By keeping sports in perspective and putting God first, young athletes can receive the fruits of His blessings. As with most worthwhile endeavors, getting started is the toughest part. A hearty work ethic and a committed attitude are essential ingredients in the ultimate success of this approach to improved athletic performance.

"HE SEARCHES AFTER EVERY GREEN"

JOB 39:8

God's Expectations

Always be joyful; never stop praying; be thankful in all circumstances, for this is God's will for you who belong to Christ Jesus.

—1 Thessalonians 5:16–18 NLT

Jesus tells us in Matthew 22:37–39 (NLT) exactly how we should live: "You must love the Lord your God with all your heart, all your soul, and all your mind. This is the first and greatest commandment. A second is equally important: Love your neighbor as yourself." That is all God asks of His children—to constantly seek a closer relationship with Him and to treat one another as they would like to be treated. By striving each day to live these ideals, our children will receive wonderful blessings from God. In John 15:4 (NIV), they are promised "Remain in Me and I will remain in you. No branch can bear fruit by itself; it must remain in the vine. Neither can you bear fruit unless you remain in Me."

Gazelle-like speed, precision hand-eye coordination, and Herculean strength are gifts from God, who wants our children to use these talents for special reasons, such as growing closer to Him and reaching others with His message. He does not want sports to fill our children with pride or create false idols that can push them away from Him. Jesus was the perfect teacher on how our children should live their lives. He stayed faithful to God's will, even when He did not want to; treated everyone with love; and gave all the glory to his heavenly Father. At the Last Supper, Jesus prayed, "Father, the time has come, Glorify your Son, that your Son may glorify you ... I have brought you glory on earth by completing the work you gave me to do" (John 17:1–4 NIV).

Athletes have a tremendous opportunity to display a positive, godly character in the arena of competition. By the way they handle winning and losing, dealing with authority, injuries, teammates, training, and all other aspects of athletics, our children can be enlightened leaders. Being all-knowing and loving, God realizes that this will not always be easy and our children will trip along the way. But He will be there to pick them up, dust them off, and guide them back onto the right path. Psalm 37:4 (NIV) tells us, "Delight yourself in the Lord and He will give you the desires of your heart."

Our society is consumed with the celebrity status of professional athletes. We honor our favorite players by wearing their jerseys. We analyze statistics for hours. We spend countless dollars on tickets, posters, clothing, memorabilia, and many other items that show our allegiance. There is nothing wrong with rooting for a team or player. Indeed there are many good men and women in professional sports who are wonderful examples of Christian living. But what about God and His son, Jesus? Do we put the same energy into honoring them? What has our child's favorite player or team done for his or her soul? Our children's happiness and salvation depends on a close relationship with God through His son, Jesus. This should be the most important relationship we encourage our children to develop—a lifetime commitment to their creator and the One who loves them unconditionally. We are told in Jonah 2:8 (NIV), "Those who cling to worthless idols forfeit the grace that could be theirs." We should not deny our children this wonderful gift.

There are other false idols that come between our children and God, such as trophies, varsity letters, team apparel, news stories, and any other items that become the focus of their attention. While it is appropriate to set goals and have dreams, our children must understand that true success and inner peace come from walking in the light of Christ. Following His will is the only way to reach the potential He has set for them. It is certainly nice to receive recognition along life's journey, but our children must not let these fleeting highlights become the purpose of their lives. After all, there would be no awards without God. Paul warns in Colossians 2:8 (NIV), "See to it that no one takes you captive through philosophy and empty deception according to the tradition of men, according to the elementary principles of the world, rather than according to Christ." Our children should enjoy the moment, whether earning a trophy or watching their favorite team win a great game, but then give the glory to their heavenly Father, who made it possible.

Jesus reinforces this message in the parable of the wise and foolish builders (Matthew 7:24–27 NIV). The wise, who built their house on rock, were protected from the fierce rain and winds, but those who built on sand could not withstand the elements. This story correlates well to our children's paths in sports and life. It is very important that they pray and listen to God's direction, practicing earnestly the virtues He inspires, as diligently as they do their sport. A combination of reverence, perseverance, and practice will ensure that our children build a strong foundation in Christ to weather any potential storms in their lives. This begins with accepting "By the grace of God I am what I am."

RIPPLES FROM THE ROCK

Social status exists in people's lives from a young age. Athletes are usually at the top of the pecking order. Conceit is a common issue that often leads to putting down other children. When this happens, it is important for someone—preferably a peer—to have the courage to step forward and change the behavior. This happens in the story "Do unto Others" when Javon, a popular kid, steps out of his comfort zone to defend another boy, Ty, against bullies who happen to be his teammates.

Do unto Others

Javon ran with the popular kids. He was blessed with good looks, an outgoing personality, and athletic abilities. He and his friends were a tight group. They sat together at lunch, hung out after school, and spent most weekends on the basketball court at the park. This particular year they were planning to try out for the Hoop Kings team, the regional travel team that had the best coaches and produced the most high school stars. Making this team had been their dream for as long as they could remember. Wearing the Hoop Kings jersey meant you were somebody in the neighborhood; the young kids looked up to you, and the older guys gave you respect as a prospect and fellow player.

Since the start of school, a new kid in the neighborhood, Ty, had been tagging along with Javon. They had many classes together. Ty was nice enough—pretty smart, actually. But he was kind of small.

"I was thinking of trying out for the Hoop Kings," Ty told Javon at lunch one day. "I know I'm not that big, but I can dribble and shoot really well, so maybe the coaches will give me a shot."

Javon encouraged his new friend. "You should definitely try out. There's nothing to lose." He smiled. "I mean, you're not on the team now, so what's the worst thing that could happen?"

One day Ty showed up at the basketball court hoping to work into a pickup game. When he came over to the group, Javon's friends ignored him.

Finally Ty said, "Hey, guys, do you have room for one more? I'm trying out for the team also and would love to work out with you."

Javon's friends were not as supportive as Javon.

Curtis scowled. "We're playing some serious ball here, kid, so you'd better step away unless you want to get hurt."

Donny was a little more direct. "You're not going to make the team, so stop wasting our time."

Ty was dejected. He had expected a better reception from fellow ballers, even if he wasn't quite at their level yet. Javon felt torn. He was one of the gang and valued his friends' approval. He also didn't want to do anything that would hurt his chances of making the team or damage his reputation around town. On the other hand, Javon knew that rejecting Ty and not letting him play was the wrong thing to do. After a few moments of awkward silence, as Ty started to walk away, Javon took action. "Hold up, guys. This is Ty—he's in some of my classes, and he's pretty cool. I say we let him play. Let's show him the ropes." The guys looked at Javon, then at Ty. Some of them didn't agree.

"C'mon, Javon," Joe-Joe complained, "there's only three weeks 'til tryouts; we don't have time to babysit someone."

Tomas piled on. "He's not going to be able to keep up, and it's going to slow the rest of us down. We can't take any chances. You know how important this team is to us."

Without another thought, the group went back to playing their game—without Ty.

Javon knew the Hoop Kings meant everything. He had waited years for his chance to try out, yet something inside told him that people were more important. He watched Ty walk away slowly, his head hanging down. Suddenly Javon felt moved to go after him. He grabbed his stuff and ran off the court as Curtis called out, "Where ya going, man? Come back; we need to finish this game."

"You guys go ahead. I'm going to practice with Ty," Javon said over his shoulder.

"Hey, Ty, wait up!" Javon fell into step with Ty and said, "I know where there is an open court we can use to shoot some hoops. You can show me that great jump shot you told me about."

Ty lifted his head and smiled. "That sounds great, Javon! But I don't want to ruin your chances of making the Hoop Kings."

"Listen," Javon said, "I can't lie. I really want to make that team, but it's not worth treating you badly. Besides, nobody has even seen you play yet, so who knows what's going to happen."

Javon had been surprised by his own actions. He was a little worried he had made the wrong decision and put his spot on the Hoop Kings in jeopardy, but at the same time he felt good about standing up for Ty.

The two boys worked out together over the next few weeks. Many of Javon's old friends were surprised to see how well Ty did at the tryouts.

"Sometimes you have to give a kid a chance," Javon explained. "I told you he had potential. You guys were so quick to dismiss him that you almost missed the opportunity of having a great new teammate and friend."

Javon made the tough choice of putting his dream at risk to treat another kid with kindness. He realized that the Hoop Kings team was not more important than friends. Javon's act of courage made a profound impact on Ty's life and was a shining example to his friends of the kind of behavior God expects from all His children.

START THE CONVERSATION

Dear Lord, help me live up to Your expectations for my life. Help me to accept Your will for my life. Help me to obey Your commandments and treat my teammates and opponents as I would like to be treated. Lord, help me to always be an example of Your love and goodness both on and off the field. Amen.

MORE GOOD NEWS: JONAH, CHAPTERS 1–3

Read the book of Jonah in the Old Testament to learn the deep meaning of God's love and discover His strong desire for all His children to follow Him. In this story, Jonah tries to run from the will of God and finds himself trapped in the belly of a whale. Eventually he repents, experiences the forgiveness and compassion of God, and goes on to fulfill the mission God intended for Him.

FIRST STEP

Before a big game or event, take the time to discuss with your child God's expectations of him or her. After the game, sit with your child to review his or her performance and attitude based on these expectations, noting where he or she reacted well and which areas of conduct need improvement.

"SHAMMAH TOOK HIS STAND IN THE MIDDLE OF THE FIELD. HE DEFENDED IT AND STRUCK THE PHILISTINES DOWN, AND THE LORD BROUGHT ABOUT A GREAT VICTORY"

2 SAMUEL 23:12

Prayer

Ask, and it will be given to you; seek, and you will find; knock, and it will be opened to you. For everyone who asks receives, and he who seeks finds, and to him who knocks it will be opened.

—Matthew 7:7–8 NAS

The most successful athletes are usually the consistent performers and those who work the hardest at their sport. The same is true with prayer. Those who pray frequently and seek the Lord constantly will reap the greatest rewards. This doesn't mean that those who pray the hardest will be the biggest winners. It is important to remember that in seeking God we are also seeking His will. At times, our children's desires and goals may be in conflict with God's purpose for them. He may want them to learn a significant lesson or set a positive example through a tough team loss or personal trying time. However, a strong faith foundation will provide our children the reward of a deep relationship with God, with whom they can share their victories and from whom they can seek strength in the face of struggles. Even Jesus prayed before He was crucified: "My Father, if it is possible, may this cup be taken from me. Yet not as I will, but as you will" (Matthew 26:39 NIV). He had to trust and believe that God knew best.

There's nothing like a good old-fashioned heart-to-heart conversation to start and strengthen a personal relationship with God. Jesus taught us that prayer is a way to speak with God. Through reading scripture and saying prayers, our children can learn about God's amazing love for them and begin to understand how much He wants to see them happy. Paul tells us, "In everything, by prayer and petition, with thanksgiving, present your requests to God. And the peace of God, which transcends all understanding, will guard your hearts and your minds in Christ Jesus" (Philippians 4:6–7 NIV). What more can we ask for our children than to see them at peace? Any healthy relationship takes work to develop. Bonding with God is no different. He longs for all His children to seek Him out and follow His will for their lives. Unfortunately, there are temptations and distractions in this world that can keep them from fully experiencing God's power and goodness. Thankfully, He sent His only son, Jesus, to show them the way. Jesus said, "If you remain in me and my words remain in you, ask whatever you wish, and it will be given you" (John 15:7 NIV).

Faith in Jesus is essential to building a lasting relationship with God. Sincere faith must be nurtured through prayer and reading scripture. In 1 Thessalonians 5:17 (NAS), Paul says, "Pray without ceasing." In Luke 6:12 (NAS), we read that Jesus Himself spent long hours in prayer: "It was at this time that He went off to the mountain to pray, and He spent the whole night in prayer to God." If Jesus spent a whole night praying to God, how much time should we spend trying to strengthen our relationship with Him? Faithful prayer takes commitment. In Jeremiah we are instructed, "Then you will call upon me and come and pray to me, and I will listen to you. You will seek me and find me when you search for me with all your heart" (Jeremiah 29:12–13 NAS).

Children might find it hard to pray when they cannot touch or hear God. However, as they read the Bible they will find many instances where Jesus encourages His disciples to let the children come to Him. With outstretched arms He invites them to experience the love of God the Father, with whom they communicate through prayer. We are promised the fruits of faith in two scriptures: "If you believe, you will receive whatever you ask for in prayer" (Matthew 21:22 NIV), and "Therefore I tell you, whatever you ask for in prayer, believe that you have received it, and it will be yours" (Mark 11:24 ESV). What powerful, encouraging words these are for our children. With such promises, they should want to pray their way onto God's team. And when they do, they will draw closer to God, bringing His peace and love into their lives.

A relationship with God is a lifetime adventure full of mystery and surprises. The sooner our children start fostering this connection, the happier and more fulfilled they will be in sports and in their lives. Whenever they feel they cannot stay the course, they need only remember "By the grace of God, I am what I am."

RIPPLES FROM THE ROCK

In "The Seeds of Faith" we meet a boy named Randy who learned how to pray at a very early age and experienced the joys that came with it. However, as he grows older and more independent, Randy relies less on prayer until a revealing situation brings it all back into focus again.

The Seeds of Faith

When Randy was very small, he would spend summers at his grandparents' farm. He loved to take early morning walks hand in hand with his Grandpa Joe.

"This is my favorite time of day," Grandpa Joe would say.

"Mine too," Randy would agree.

Though they never followed the same path twice, these two adventurers always seemed to find themselves sitting on the big rock ledge overlooking the stream that ran along the edge of the farm.

After a few quiet moments enjoying their surroundings, Grandpa Joe would say, "Dear Lord, thank You for the beautiful sunrise that greeted us this morning. Thank You for the chirping birds that provide such a sweet serenade. Thank You for the spotted deer drinking from the stream below, and thank You for my wonderful grandson Randy."

Then Randy would chime in. "God, thank You for helping me catch my first fish yesterday. Thank You for not letting me drown when I jumped off the tire swing into the stream. Thank You for those delicious chocolate-chip cookies Grandma made, and thank You for my wonderful Grandpa Joe!"

One day while they were walking back to the house, Randy asked Grandpa Joe why he spent so much time talking to God and thanking Him.

"Well," Grandpa Joe said, "before placing my needs and intentions before God, I make sure to thank Him for all the blessings He has already given me. It reminds me that even though I may still be waiting for God to answer certain prayers, I still have so much to be thankful for if I just take the time to look around."

Randy picked up a stone and skimmed it along the water.

"You really trust God a lot, Grandpa," he observed.

"I certainly do, Randy, and He hasn't let me down yet!"

Randy felt fortunate to spend so many of his younger days with his grandpa, who brought him closer to God. Slowly, though, things changed. Randy grew older and became more involved with school friends and activities. In the summer, he attended camps and worked, so he could not spend as much time with Grandpa Joe. Losing that daily influence, and falling into the trap of popularity and busyness, Randy didn't pray as often as before. Everything from sports to studies seemed to come easily to him, so he thought he had it all under control. He was the premier quarterback in the youth football league. Then one day before a big game, he noticed a player on the other team walk off to the side, take a knee, and silently pray.

The game was a defensive battle between two powerhouse programs. Randy was not only the quarterback but also led the defense from his middle linebacker position.

"No more first downs!" Randy screamed at his teammates. "Stick 'em at the line of scrimmage. We have to hold them here."

Randy's team was down by a point with little time left on the clock. They needed to stop their opponents and get the ball back for one last chance to score. Randy's defense came through, and his team took over possession of the ball. On their first play, Randy was sacked for a six-yard loss. In the huddle after the play, Randy let his linemen have an earful.

"What's wrong with you guys? I can't win this game myself. You guys have to block better so I can make the play. Get your act together!"

On second down Randy dropped back to pass again, but the result was no different—another sack.

"You guys are terrible!" he screamed. "Don't you want to win? How about blocking for once?"

"We're trying our best, Randy," center Dwight Shultz said. "They're just too big and strong."

"Well, your best isn't good enough," Randy shot back. "If we lose this game, it won't be my fault."

Third down was a little better, but the team only got back to the original line of scrimmage. That left enough time for one last play on fourth down. With little choice, Coach Brewers sent in a trick play to try to score the winning touchdown.

"Don't screw this up, guys," Randy sneered as he gave his teammates the play. "If we do this right, their left cornerback will be fooled and Danny will be wide open in the end zone."

Randy executed the play brilliantly, and his team pulled off a dramatic victory.

The cornerback caught out of position was devastated. People in the stands were screaming, even cursing at him. Some of his teammates were shaking their heads and blaming him for the loss. As Randy was celebrating, he noticed the boy who had been praying before the game walk over to his dejected teammate and put his arm around his shoulder. Although he could not hear their conversation, he could tell by his manner that he was consoling and bolstering his teammate. Shortly after, they crossed the field together, and before too long they were smiling. That scene made a big impact on Randy. He realized he was so caught up with winning and his own personal performance that he had become a bad teammate and a not-so-nice person. Yet this quarterback of the losing team, who could have joined in blaming his teammate, chose instead to console his friend. He had something special about him, and it dawned on Randy that it was prayer, as well as the grace that comes from a daily relationship with God. Suddenly Grandpa Joe's voice and words of wisdom flooded back to Randy and his heart opened to embrace it.

Starting that day, Randy reconnected with God and prayer became the thread connecting everything in his life. He began to pray openly before and after every game. Influenced by Randy's improved attitude, some teammates began to join him in prayer, and together they played for the glory of God. Now in his senior year, Randy has plenty of decisions facing him, such as where to go to college, what to study, and whether to try out for a team. These can be stressful times, but Randy feels content knowing that God is on his side and will guide him along the right path. His years of playing sports have helped him to work hard and set goals for himself, always remembering to pray along the way.

START THE CONVERSATION

Dear Lord, I place myself in Your hands today. I ask You to guide me on the right paths and give me the courage, strength, and ability to do my best in all situations. Help me to let You shine through me in my thoughts, actions, and accomplishments. I believe that nothing is impossible with You, my God, beside me!

MORE GOOD NEWS: DANIEL, CHAPTER 6

In this story, Daniel stays faithful to God in spite of a royal decree forbidding any worship other than to King Darius. Daniel ignores the order and continues his daily prayer to God. When this results in Daniel being thrown in the lion's den, God prevents any harm from coming to Daniel and thus transforms the lives of not only Daniel but King Darius as well.

FIRST STEP

Encourage your child to begin each day by talking with God. Have him or her speak out loud—in his or her room or another quiet place—and share whatever he or she is thinking or feeling. Suggest that your child picture God in the room with him or her. Have your child say good morning and tell Him what he or she expects to happen during the day. Let Him know his or her worries and fears. Have your child ask God to stick with him or her all day long. Gradually your child can incorporate this conversation-style prayer into his or her pregame warm-ups. During these times your child can talk to God in his or her head and always picture Him right there beside him or her.

"I WILL ASCEND ABOVE THE HEIGHTS
OF THE CLOUDS"

ISAIAH 14:14

Godliness

He said to him, "You shall love the Lord your God with all your heart, and with all your soul, and with all your mind. This is the great and foremost commandment. The second is like it, you shall love your neighbor as yourself."

—Matthew 22:37–39 NAS

We should all strive to lead godly lives. This means treating others with kindness and respect; valuing all people, even opponents; and putting God's will above our own. Youth sports provide a great training ground for helping our children develop these traits. Primarily, they need to understand that while sports may be their passion, being a godly person is most important. In 1 Timothy 4:8 (ESV), we read, "For while bodily training is of some value, godliness is of value in every way, as it holds promise for the present life and also for the life to come." There are many opportunities on the fields, courts, and tracks of life for children to let their actions speak of God. Through acts of courage, humility, determination, and kindness, our young athletes can become role models to others.

The Bible is an essential ingredient to this approach, giving our children the nuggets of wisdom they need to model godly behavior in their lives. Paul tells us in 2 Timothy 3:16–17 (NLT), "All Scripture is inspired by God and is useful to teach us what is true and to make us realize what is wrong in our lives. It corrects us when we are wrong and teaches us to do what is right. God uses it to prepare and equip his people to do every good work."

Through scripture reading, prayer, and a personal relationship with God, our children will become more balanced, more accepting, more appreciative, and more confident. They will come to understand God's power and goodness and His desire to see them happy. Peter explains in 2 Peter 1:3 (NIV) that "His divine power has given us everything we need for life and godliness through our knowledge of Him who called us by his own glory and goodness." Trusting God in the athletic arena will train our children to do the same in larger life matters.

Maintaining a godly attitude can be difficult in the face of stiff competition. Under pressure, young athletes can lose their temper, blame teammates for mistakes, and abandon their principles for poor sportsmanship. It takes courage, conviction, and a certain amount of confidence for them to stay true to their values under these circumstances. There are times when our children will meet resistance from their peers or even coaches and other parents. However, Paul provides encouragement in 1 Corinthians 16:13–14 (NIV): "Be on your guard; stand firm in the faith; be men of courage; be strong. Do everything in love." If our children radiate God's love in all their words and actions, no matter the circumstances, they will receive inner strength and demonstrate godly behavior to others. This is the essential message that Jesus brought to us.

It is okay to compete aggressively. Yet, by taking a godly approach, our children can seek victory wholeheartedly while still embracing sportsmanship and fair play. This involves humbly maximizing their athletic ability, giving all glory to God, and staying faithful to His "code of conduct." Micah 6:8 (NAS) illustrates how God calls our children to live: "He has told you, O man, what is good; and what does the Lord require of you but to do justice, and to love kindness, and to walk humbly with your God." This is valuable advice for every aspect of life. Demonstrating godliness in all circumstances, athletic and otherwise, will lead our children closer to God and the blessings He will pour out upon them. Paul promises in 1 Timothy 6:6 (NIV), "Godliness with contentment is great gain." The first step is realizing "By the grace of God, I am what I am."

RIPPLES FROM THE ROCK

In this story we learn what it means to be godly through the actions of a group of young boys on a baseball field. These boys understand the true meaning of winning and sportsmanship. Read "The Hands of Hope" and see how the Spirit of Christ touched so many lives during one Little League game.

The Hands of Hope

It was an ideal spring morning for baseball. The grass was freshly cut. The sun warmed the infield clay to a perfect consistency. And the undefeated Orange Crush were warming up in the outfield.

"We're really playing well," Coach Phillips said as he looked over the lineup. He smiled at his assistant. "The way the whole team is contributing, I believe I could put any nine players on the field and we would just keep winning."

As the boys came running into the dugout, ace pitcher Aidan McMurphy smiled at coach Phillips. "Am I starting today? I haven't given up a run in my last three games, and I am feeling great today!"

"You're the man!" Coach Phillips shot back. "We're going to ride your arm all the way to the championship this year."

As the managers met at home plate to exchange lineup cards, Coach Peterson of the opposing Blue Stingrays spoke quietly to Coach Phillips. "I need a big favor today, Philly." The two coaches knew each other from around town and respected each other.

"What's on your mind, Peety? Want me to take it easy on you guys today?" Coach Phillips teased.

"Actually, it's more than that, Don," Coach Peterson said seriously. "I have an outstanding young man on my team named Charlie. He hasn't missed a practice or game all season. He also hasn't been on base all year."

"Sounds like the Stingrays need a new coach," Phillips chided.

"Well, I am sure some folks would agree with you, but this is a special case. Charlie is autistic. I really want to do something special for this kid. He is such a great teammate, and the boys on my team have really accepted him as a friend and fellow Stingray. They have never complained, even though he is an automatic out every time he comes up to bat."

"Sounds like you have done a remarkable job with your squad, Tom," Coach Phillips said.

"I would like to see Charlie get on base today, Don," Coach Peterson blurted out. "He won't swing the bat when he's at the plate, but would you mind walking him? I'm telling you, it will mean the world to him."

"No problem," Coach Phillips replied. "Let me go talk with my team and get them on the same page. Just give me a sign when Charlie comes up to bat, and we will take care of the rest."

Back in the Orange Crush dugout, Coach Phillips addressed his team. "At some point in this game, a young man is going to come up to bat for the Stingrays and we are going to walk him."

"What are you talking about, Coach?" Billy Adams asked.

Coach Phillips shared the conversation he'd had with Coach Peterson and asked if anyone on the team had a problem with the promise he had made to his friend and fellow coach.

They all nodded, and Aidan McMurphy chimed in. "Just let me know when he comes up, and I will walk him."

Pleased with the positive response of his team, Coach Phillips shouted, "Let's play ball!"

It was the third inning when Charlie finally came to the plate. Since Aidan was such a talented pitcher, he was able to walk Charlie without making it look too obvious. Pitch after pitch came in—too high or low, in the dirt or out of the zone; but close enough that nobody in the crowd grew suspicious. On ball four, Charlie tossed his bat and ran toward first base, beaming from ear to ear. The crowd cheered loudly. Charlie's mom could not contain her excitement and ran from the bleachers to snap a picture of her boy.

Moved by the moment, catcher Thomas Bittman called time out and walked out to the mound to speak with Aidan.

"You know, it might be cool if we let him score," he whispered.

Aidan was taken aback by his friend's suggestion.

"C'mon, man. You know I haven't given up a run in three games. If I hold the Stingrays scoreless in this game, I will break the league record," Aidan protested.

Soon all the infielders were standing around the pitcher's mound talking. Coach Phillips knew something serious was being discussed but for some reason felt it best to let the boys handle it themselves.

Robby Morris, the quick and athletic shortstop, spoke up. "Look, Aidan, it's your record, and you're the one throwing the balls in there, so the decision is yours, but I think Thomas is right. We have many more years to make memories. Who knows how much longer Charlie will be playing ball? This may be the only chance he ever has to cross home plate."

"You can groove some nice pitches over the plate and let the Stingrays get a few hits until Charlie scores," third baseman Juan Martinez interjected.

The umpire walked toward the meeting taking place in the middle of the field and said, "Break it up, boys. Batter up."

The boys ran back to their positions, and Aidan rolled the baseball around in his hand as he contemplated his next move. Aidan was all for walking Charlie, but letting him score was going to take a bigger sacrifice than maybe he was willing to make. That scoreless games record would sure be nice to add to his collection. Aidan glared in at the next batter and blew one of his signature fastballs right by him for strike one. As the catcher threw the ball back to Aidan, Charlie took off for second base. Lost in his own thoughts, Aidan didn't see the steal, and Charlie wound up safe at second. The crowd went wild. Charlie's mom and dad were jumping up and down with excitement watching their son run the bases.

Suddenly Aidan realized this moment was much bigger than him and his record. He recalled all the games where his parents had cheered with pride at his many successes. He knew this was Charlie's moment. His teammates were right. Charlie had to score. The next pitch Aidan threw was right down the middle, and it was lined to center field for a base hit. Charlie moved to third base, where Coach Peterson greeted him with a high five.

"Way to go, Charlie! Wait until I tell you to run and then sprint home," he instructed.

The next batter dug in, and Aidan grooved another pitch right over the plate. The Stingrays' cleanup hitter drove the ball deep to left field, way over the head of the Orange Crush fielder.

"Run!" Coach Peterson screamed.

"Get home!" Charlie's teammates shouted.

Charlie took off, and as he crossed home plate his teammates rushed the field and surrounded him in a joyous celebration. Watching the Stingrays celebrate as if they had won the championship confirmed to Aidan that he had done the right thing.

After shutting down the Stingrays to end the inning with only the one run scoring, Aidan headed to the dugout. Coach Phillips met him at the edge of the field.

"I am so proud of you," he said. "I know it was not easy for you to let that run score. You showed great leadership out there. With that kind of character, you certainly have a bright future both on and off the field."

Aidan smiled and said, "Thanks, Coach."

When the game was over, Coach Peterson approached the Orange Crush huddle.

"I want you boys to know how proud I am of you all," he said.

"What do you mean?" Angel Garcia asked. "We beat you fifteen to one."

Coach Peterson explained. "The final score doesn't mean anything in the game of life. I asked your coach to walk one of my players so he could experience the thrill of making it to first base. I never imagined you boys would take it upon yourselves to let him score. That was a very classy thing to do, and it took courage and heart to pull it off. I hope you boys win the championship this year, but either way, you are all champions in my book."

Trophies collect dust and get relegated to closet corners through the years. However, impacting the soul of another human being is something we carry in our hearts for life. Aidan, Charlie, and their teammates, as well as the coaches and parents in the dugouts and bleachers, will long remember what happened that day when they witnessed God at work on the baseball field.

START THE CONVERSATION

Prayer of St. Francis of Assisi

Lord, make me an instrument of your peace. Where there is hatred, let me sow love; where there is injury, pardon; where there is doubt, faith; where there is despair, hope; where there is darkness, light; and where there is sadness, joy.

O Divine Master, grant that I may not so much seek to be consoled as to console; to be understood as to understand; to be loved as to love. For it is in giving that we receive; it is in pardoning that we are pardoned; and it is in dying that we are born to eternal life.

Amen.

MORE GOOD NEWS: LUKE 10:25–37

Jesus taught us to love our neighbors as ourselves. Doing the right thing is not always easy, but in the parable of the good Samaritan we are reminded that reaching out to others with compassion, understanding, and love—even when it is not socially acceptable—is what we are called to do.

FIRST STEP

Encourage your child to volunteer for a good cause—one that calls him or her to action on behalf of others. Whatever the outreach, your child should incorporate it into his or her regular schedule to ensure he or she is always thinking of others and acting in a godly way.

"FORGETTING WHAT IS BEHIND AND STRAINING TOWARD WHAT IS AHEAD, I PRESS ON TOWARD THE GOAL TO WIN THE PRIZE."

PHILIPPIANS 3:13

Hard Work

But by the grace of God I am what I am, and his grace toward me was not in vain. On the contrary, I worked harder than any of them, though it was not I, but the grace of God that is with me.

—1 Corinthians 15:10 ESV

When it comes to sports, hard work is expected. Even the youngest athletes learn that the only way to improve performance is by practicing and pushing the limits of comfort. Tapping into their inner rock requires the same dedication to hard work on the part of our children. Sometimes getting to God means cracking through a tough exterior, so a lot of focused strength is necessary to make the connection. Abundant blessings will flow from our heavenly Father to those children who have a personal relationship with Him. Just as with any other relationship, the more each party is willing to work and commit, the stronger the bond will be. We know that God's goodness is perfect and constant, so the real effort has to come from our side. James 2:26 (NAS) explains that faith and work go hand in hand: "For just as the body without the spirit is dead, so also faith without works is dead."

Our children must not only exert effort in strengthening their faith but must also work hard at fulfilling God's will. They may have dreams of playing on a certain team or achieving a certain goal, but as they open themselves to God's will it may turn out that He has something else planned for them. This can be hard to accept, and waiting is especially difficult for children. However, God's plan is usually revealed over time, and if they work hard to seek it, our children will find true happiness. The hardest work begins when our children accept God's plan for them and strive to carry it out to the fullest of their potential. Solomon states, "Whatever your hand finds to do, do it with all your might" (Ecclesiastes 9:10 NAS). This is how they truly glorify God and keep the relationship strong.

God made it clear from the beginning that He would shower His children with blessings but they would be required to work hard to experience the joy of His promises fully. God created paradise in Eden, but Adam had to work the land. "The Lord God took the man and put him in the Garden of Eden to work it and keep it" (Genesis 2:15 ESV). Adam could not just lounge around playing video games. In order to fully experience God's goodness, he had to take care of the land and use the gifts God gave him to be a good steward of the garden. Similarly, our children need to spend time practicing and developing their God-given abilities. They glorify God by accepting His gifts and maximizing their impact through hard work. Just as Adam had to work hard caring for the garden of Eden, so our children should put tremendous effort into tending the talents God has given them. This means they must commit themselves to the rigors of training and practice. They cannot show up on race day expecting to win the 5K based on faith alone. Solomon provides good counsel in this regard: "The sluggard craves and gets nothing, but the desires of the diligent are fully satisfied" (Proverbs 13:4 NIV).

It is clear that in addition to developing a strong faith in God, our children must nurture a proper work ethic in order to reach their full potential. Forging a close relationship with God will deepen their faith and provide the endurance necessary to carry out His will. By discerning God's will and working hard to execute it, our children will bring Him glory. And when they bring glory to God, He will certainly bless their lives. The process begins by embracing the fact that "by the grace of God, I am what I am."

RIPPLES FROM THE ROCK

Living in a culture of instant gratification, many children can find it difficult to work at a long-term goal. In the story "Delayed Dream," a young boy struggles between giving up his dream or putting in extra time and hard work and trusting God with the results.

Delayed Dream

Thump ... thump ... thump—a sound that has been as regular as the ticking clock in Thomas's house since he was four years old. Well, more like against Thomas's house. He practiced lacrosse moves every free moment of the day (and night). When he wasn't thumping the ball, he was twisting his stick and honing his maneuvers. He played on his local team and never missed a clinic. Thomas lived and breathed lacrosse. Now he was ten and *finally* able to try out for a regional tournament team.

"Earth to Thomas ... are you there, Thomas?" The sound of his mom's voice calling from the window snapped him out of his daydream. In it, Thomas was decked out in pads and a black-and-gold uniform, doing some fancy tricks with his stick.

I'm going to ace tryouts, I can just feel it, he thought to himself while heading in for dinner.

Over the next few weeks, Thomas practiced every free minute he had. He found it hard to concentrate at school; all he wanted to do was to play lacrosse.

Tryouts were packed! Many of his friends—and biggest rivals—were there. Thomas felt nervous but confident. He was able to keep up with the other guys and seemed capable of executing what the coaches were asking them to do. Three hours passed as the coaches ran the kids through drills and a scrimmage. He was sweaty but happy when it ended.

"We'll be in touch within the week," Coach Francis, the team coordinator, told them.

Waiting was hard, so to take his mind off it, Thomas played ... lacrosse. He couldn't help imagining the first game and all the fun he would have over the season.

When the phone rang Friday night, Thomas's mom picked it up, "Hello, Coach."

He watched his mom nod her head a couple of times and then clear her throat. "I see ... really?" She passed the phone to him with a "my poor baby" look.

Thomas's heart fell when he heard the words "Thomas, you had a great tryout. We could all tell how hard you worked, and we do see a lot of potential. The thing is, you can use a little more speed and some seasoning. We know you are disappointed, Thomas, but please don't give up. Keep playing and taking those clinics; we want to see you at tryouts next year. Good-bye, son."

"Bye ..." Thomas hung up the phone, fighting the tears pounding behind his eyes.

He ran hard through the living room and out into the garage, slamming the door behind him. All he wanted to do was break his lacrosse stick in two and bury his head under a pillow. "All that work for nothing! When will I ever be good enough!" he screamed to nobody in particular, cutting his stick viciously through the air. Finally he hurled it to the ground and fell alongside it, huffing and puffing. No more dreams—just a hard reality to face.

His family tried to cheer him up over the next few days, but Thomas walked around with an angry face and bad attitude. He wouldn't even look at his stick in the garage. Mad thoughts raced through his mind. He thought about quitting, giving it all up, but after a week he started missing the rhythm of tossing the ball and catching it in his net.

One night his dad came into his room and sat on the edge of the bed. "Thomas, this has been a tough time for you, we know. Not everything in life turns out the way we plan. You have to ask yourself some questions. The biggest one being, do you want to stick with lacrosse? If so, how are you going to move forward? If not, what's next?"

The following week, his dad took him to a nearby college lacrosse expo. It was the first twinge of excitement he had felt in weeks.

There were many learning opportunities and interesting people to meet at the expo. As a treat his dad took him to a customizing booth where he picked out a gold net and watched the man string it on his favorite stick. They sat in on several demonstrations and had the chance to ask questions of some high-level college lacrosse players and coaches. He even got a few autographs to hang up on his bedroom wall. The highlight of his day was a hands-on clinic, where he joined a group of kids his age for warm-ups and a scrimmage with an all-star roster of lacrosse players. The guys were really down-to-earth and fun.

At the end of the game, the players called them all into a huddle to hear one senior's inspiring story. He told them how he had played lacrosse all through high school and was being recruited by many colleges. Humbly he went on to say that he made some wrong choices his senior year, which resulted in a suspension from the team. Hearing about it, the college that had offered him a full scholarship said they would have to reconsider. He had spent the next three months in limbo—riding the bench and wondering if his current coach and the college coach would change their minds. During that time, a friend introduced him to God and he began to develop a deep prayer life. He still practiced lacrosse every day and worked out to stay in shape, but he also put a lot of time into reading the Bible and learning more about his faith. He began to listen better—to his parents, his coaches, and, most of all, to God. He realized that this time of punishment was really a time for him to take a closer look at himself. Rather than be anxious about whether he would be able to play again, he started thinking about how he could live a better life. He took responsibility for the mistakes he made and apologized to the people whom he had either hurt or disappointed. Eventually, his suspension was lifted, but the spot at his first-choice college was no longer open. Disappointed, but newly inspired to accept God's plan for his life, this young man was led to a smaller college with the opportunity to play lacrosse for them. He ended his story by telling the boys that making a wrong decision actually led him to the right path and reminding them to stay open to the possibilities in their lives, even if things aren't always going according to their own personal plans.

This young man's story struck a deep chord with Thomas. His dad's words came flooding back to him, and he realized that yes, he did still want to play lacrosse. He thought about his recent frustrations and anger, and began to see things in a different light. Like this young man, he had been learning lessons through the tough times. He realized that this would mean a change of attitude. The guy he had just listened to showed him that there is a lot more to playing than handling the stick. Something changed inside of him, and he felt a new sense of hope.

Spring came calling through Thomas's window. Once again he twisted his stick, and to his family's relief, the house started thumping again. Following his own reflections and the inspiring story of the college lacrosse player he had met, Thomas began to seek out God's will. He realized that quitting was not the answer, so he went to work, practicing and conditioning even harder than before, and added another dimension to his training—prayer.

One day he called Coach Francis for some tips. "Hello, Coach, it's Thomas Parker. I was wondering if you could give me some drills to practice so I can get in the best possible shape for next year's tryouts."

"That's a great approach, Thomas. Come by the field tomorrow afternoon, and I'll have some exercises and drills written up for you. I can even give you a little demonstration," Coach responded happily.

With a new at-home regimen and a fresh commitment to his local team, Thomas put forth 110 percent effort the rest of the season and all through the next year. He watched high school and college games, read whatever he could about lacrosse, prayed often, and committed himself to making the tournament team one day.

Thomas's passion and dedication paid off—eventually. He did not make the tournament team at age eleven, but that didn't stop him. He continued on his positive path and was overjoyed when Coach Francis called after the twelve-year-old tryouts to say he had made the team. He will never take anything for granted in his life, because through his lacrosse trials and disappointments, Thomas learned that it takes hard work, discipline, faith, and passion to make one's dreams come true.

START THE CONVERSATION

Dear Jesus, today I begin asking for Your help in doing all the things on my list to the best of my ability. You carried a heavy cross and never complained. I will keep that in mind as I do my drills, homework, and chores so that every time I feel like giving up I remember how little this is compared to how much You sacrificed. Thank You, Jesus, for all You did and all You continue to do in my life.

MORE GOOD NEWS: ACTS 20:17–38

Standing up for your beliefs requires strength, courage, and a lot of prayer. Paul called all of these into action during his three years in Asia, where he proclaimed Christ's teachings to many unbelievers and suffered because of it. Yet he stayed strong and, when he was ready to leave for another land, encouraged his followers to do the same—to work hard and live purposefully without being caught up in the material trappings of the world—in the name of Jesus.

FIRST STEP

Have your child create a practice, homework, chore, and prayer calendar outlining appropriate times for each activity throughout the week. Display the calendar in a prominent place so your child can refer to it every day. Have your child track his or her progress on meeting goals for each area of work. You can also designate certain little rewards as targeted goals are met.

"STRENGTHEN YOUR FEEBLE ARMS
AND WEAK KNEES"

HEBREWS 12:12 (NIV)

Commitment / Perseverance

For whatever was written in earlier times was written for our instruction, so that through perseverance and the encouragement of the Scriptures we might have hope.

—Romans 15:4 NAS

Commitment to anything can be a struggle; it is as important to faith as it is to sports, and it requires both determination and willpower. As our children navigate the world of competitive sports, it is important for them to understand that their personal goals and timing may be different from God's vision for them. This is why it is critical to commit to both physical training and, most important, to deepening their relationship with God. They need to understand that accepting and committing to God's will is not always easy. In Hebrews 10:36 (NIV), Paul explains, "You need to persevere so that when you have done the will of God you will receive what He has promised."

Teaching children about commitment is best done by example. Commitment is about being there and giving of ourselves for someone or something in which we believe. As parents, we demonstrate a commitment to family by making time for our children and providing for their needs. We show a commitment to our jobs by being hardworking and reliable employees. In our churches, we show commitment by giving of our talents and treasures. Through active community service, we show a commitment to our local towns. Paul told the Galatians in 6:9 (NIV), "Let us not become weary in doing good, for at the proper time we will reap a harvest if we do not give up."

Most children understand that a commitment to regular practice will improve their performance. It is vital that they put the same energy into prayer, Bible study, and quiet listening so they can begin to hear God's plan. This commitment to tapping their inner rock will yield additional benefits, making them enlightened athletes who are prepared to handle any situation with athletic prowess and God's graces. "Blessed is the man who remains steadfast under trial, for when he has stood the test he will receive the crown of life, which God has promised to those who love him" (James 1:12 ESV).

We must encourage our children to practice their faith just as much as their sport. They need to work on strengthening their relationship with God constantly, with each step bringing them to a greater realization of His pivotal role in their lives—in sports and beyond. This begins with accepting "By the grace of God, I am what I am."

RIPPLES FROM THE ROCK

Some people can get inspired and be inspiring all at once. This is the case with Caela, a teenager we meet in the story "The Last Shall Be First." Not particularly athletic, Caela joins a sport that requires intense endurance, and she commits to it for four years. Read how the experience changed her life and impacted the lives of her teammates.

The Last Shall Be First

September was only two months away. It marked the start of high school and, Caela promised herself, a new attitude. Socially shy, Caela never participated in after-school activities or inserted herself into new situations. Feeling a little removed from her peers, she decided to make some changes. The question was where to begin.

"Why don't you try the cross-country team?" her mom's friend suggested. "My son had such a good experience doing that. It's a great group of people, and they start practicing over the summer, so you meet kids before school starts."

Caela had never run, or done any sport for that matter. God had given her many blessings, but she accepted that athleticism was not among them. She preferred a book or good movie to exercise. Although the thought of running every day during the hot summer months was not appealing, she did like the idea of becoming part of a group and meeting new people.

After prayerful consideration, Caela announced to her parents, "I think I'm going to see what cross-country is all about."

The first practice was exhausting—every muscle in her body ached that night—but she was intrigued. The girls were really nice, and she always did like a challenge. Soon the daily practices became part of her summer routine; in fact, they were the highlight of each day for her. Little by little, Caela built muscle and endurance, so by the time school started she was in shape for tryouts and made the team.

"I'm probably the slowest girl out there, but it doesn't bother me," Caela explained to her parents. "Everyone is so encouraging, especially Coach Hendricks. He really believes in all of us and helps us set our personal goals. My goal is to finish every race this season."

Everyone was excited and nervous about the first meet. Fifty or sixty girls in various school colors with numbers pinned to their jerseys met at the starting line. Suddenly the pistol fired and they were off, swarming across the green field like honeybees, each falling into her own pace. Caela fell to the back of the pack but kept her steady pace, recalling all the pointers Coach Hendricks had made during practices. Along the path, her teammates called out to each other: "That's it, Julia, you got it"; "Keep going, Caela; breathe easy!" Even girls from other teams threw out words of encouragement—usually as they were passing her, but still, it was so nice. At mile two, she felt a cramp coming on and stooped over to work through it.

The next thing she knew, a breathless but caring voice told her, "Work thought it, Caela, the end is in sight ... It's just a cramp; it'll go away. Come on, follow me!" It was Jamie, and those few words were like medicine. The cramp stopped, and Caela felt motivated to follow her friend.

Many, many girls had passed her along the way, and Caela knew she was at the end of the pack. But she was so inspired as she passed each marker and realized she was getting close to the finish line. "I'm almost there," she told herself over and over, stride after stride. Suddenly it got noisier; people were lining up along the final stretch, clapping and calling her name.

"Go, Caela!"

"C'mon, girl, you've got this!"

"Look, the finish line is in sight; kick it in!"

One by one, her teammates Molly, Jessica, Kim, Haley, and Melissa cheered her along. They were red-faced and sweaty, having finished the race and run back to show their support. It was exhilarating! Their encouragement propelled her the last several hundred yards and carried her over the finish line. Breathless, she fell to her knees, taking in the scene. Two months before, she would never have imagined that she could complete a 5K race. Today she learned a lot about her inner self and felt new confidence.

Cross-country was a big part of Caela's high school years; many would say she was the heart of the team. Consistently in last place, she never begrudged the lead runners or hung her head in frustration. Instead, she wore a ready smile, was a supportive teammate, and kept her steady pace, putting everything she had into every race. Many of her nonrunner friends would ask Caela why she put herself through those grueling workouts and endless miles only to come in last place time after time. Why didn't she join something where she would excel? But what they couldn't understand, and what Caela came to learn as time unfolded, was that winning is not always the ultimate goal. God leads us all down different paths for different reasons, and if we are open to His plan and stay committed to our faith, we will find special treasures. In Caela's case, she found confidence, friendship, and endurance—gifts that will last a lifetime. Through her witness she also became a model of acceptance and courage for her teammates and coach.

In a fitting tribute to her during Senior Night, a teammate said, "Caela has been an inspiration for this whole team. Her commitment, positive attitude, and humility have shown us all that winning isn't about the best time; it's about putting your best foot forward day after day, race after race. If loyalty and perseverance are the keys to success, Caela has a bright future. We will miss her, but there is no doubt that her legacy will live on in the spirit of our cross-country team."

What started as a quest to make friends became a journey of self-discovery for Caela. With college on the horizon, she could be confident that whatever challenges came her way, she had the inner faith and fortitude to face them and succeed.

START THE CONVERSATION

Dear Lord, I dedicate this day and my workout to You. Help me to grow in faith, perseverance, and understanding. Teach me to honor my commitments, and give me the desire to grow ever deeper in my relationship with You.

MORE GOOD NEWS: DANIEL, CHAPTER 3

Imagine being thrown into a burning furnace and coming out without a mark. This is what happened to three men of Babylon when they refused to worship the king's golden statue. These men were committed to their belief in the one true God, so the king, in a fit of rage, had them tossed into a fiery furnace. While inside they continued to utter praises to God, and so He sent an angel to protect them from the flames. Their deep faith and conviction brought saving grace and caused the king to open his eyes to new ways of thinking.

FIRST STEP

Have your child commit to a morning or evening workout routine in which he or she develops a ten-to-fifteen-minute program of physical and spiritual exercises. Have your child keep a journal of how he or she feels before and after this workout. Review with your child weekly how his or her commitment to this program is improving his or her physical and spiritual well-being.

"I AM AMONG YOU AS THE ONE WHO SERVES."

LUKE 22:27

Balance / Perspective

Do not conform yourself to this age but be transformed by the renewal of your mind, that you may discern what is the will of God, what is good and pleasing and perfect.

—Romans 12:2 NAS

Participation in sports programs can have a positive impact on our children's development. Through such programs, they learn to be physically fit, deal with different personalities, handle pressure situations, and value hard work, among other things. These virtues can pay dividends over the course of their lifetimes. However, it is important they understand that participating in sports is only one dimension of their lives. The key is to help our children find balance between sports and life, and develop a healthy perspective about where they fit into God's bigger picture. God delights in seeing His children use the athletic talents He has given them. He also calls them to use these gifts for greater good; to give Him all the glory in success and to seek His purpose for their whole life—not just the sports portion of it. To this end, Matthew 6:33 (NLT) says, "Seek the Kingdom of God above all else, and live righteously, and he will give you everything you need."

It is difficult not to get caught up in the drama and excitement of the sports scene. After all, family calendars are filled with hours of practices, games, meets, and competitions. We often sacrifice the pleasure of attending family functions and even skip church for the sake of getting to games. Sports become all-consuming. When our children realize that someone bigger, stronger, wiser, and more loving than them—or anyone else—is in charge, they gain a broader perspective about life. No matter the level of success they may reach in sports, taking a God-centered approach will enable them to find balance and develop an important perspective that can be shared with others.

Consider the gifted quarterback or agile point guard who refrains from beating his or her chest following an amazing pass or three-pointer. Instead, the player shares the glory with his or her teammates, knowing that everyone plays a role in the end result. They also give thanks to God for the talent that enables them to accomplish such feats. These kids have balance. On the other hand, there are situations in which one player tries to steal the show, making the game all about him or her. There are kids who question every referee's call and storm off when things don't go their way. These players have lost perspective. Matthew 16:26 (NIV) explains, "What good will it be if a man gains the whole world, yet forfeits his soul? Or what can a man give in exchange for his soul?" Turning to prayer and the Bible for the truth about God and His son, Jesus, is a wonderful approach for young athletes. Feeding the soul will have a positive effect on the body and overall performance.

Sports should not consume our children's lives. There will come a day when they wear their uniforms for the last time. They must have the perspective to take the many lessons they have learned through sports and apply them to the rest of their lives. That is why the first team our children should aspire to be on is God's team. On God's team there are no cuts, everyone gets more than enough playing time, and each player has a lifetime contract. With God as their head coach, the victory will be sweet. By accepting God's plan and trusting His power and goodness in *every* aspect of their lives, our children give honor and glory to God while keeping the role of sports in perspective. Paul tells us in Colossians 3:17 (NAS), "Whatever you do in word or deed, do all in the name of the Lord Jesus, giving thanks through Him to God the Father."

Armed with this knowledge, as well as the athletic abilities God has granted them, our children become vehicles of a precious message and can enlighten people around them. Second Timothy 2:15 (NAS) explains, "Be eager to present yourself as acceptable to God, a workman who causes no disgrace, imparting the word of truth without deviation." Our children can best accomplish this by accepting "By the grace of God. I am what I am."

RIPPLES FROM THE ROCK

One of the most difficult things any athlete can face is an injury, as this can cause his or her hopes for a season to come crashing down, with the thought of sitting on the bench. This happens to Mel, a talented, goal-oriented volleyball player. In "A Change of Heart," she goes through a range of emotions and actions as she grapples with her bad news and figures out how she will ultimately handle what is out of her control.

A Change of Heart

This isn't good, Mel thought as pain seared through her hand and arm following a hard spike over the net. She scored the point but fell to the floor in agony. The game stopped, and Coach Rayburn ran onto the court and squatted beside her while the other players took a knee.

"Let me take a look at that, Mel," he said quietly.

"It's fine. I just need some ice, and I'll be okay for the next set," she replied outwardly, but in her head Mel cried, *My arm is the size of a watermelon, and I feel like I'm going to pass out from the pain.*

"Jen, go in for Mel," Coach called as he guided Mel to the bench.

For the rest of the game, Mel soaked her arm and watched her team lose its lead to the Muskrats, their biggest rival. *Man, I want to be out there,* Mel thought furiously. But for her there was nowhere to go but the emergency room, where she discovered that her arm was fractured in two areas and that she needed surgery.

It was early in the season, yet Mel's road to recovery was long and her patience was thin. Day after day as she sat on the bench watching other girls take her spot, Mel fumed quietly.

"I cannot believe Veronica messed up that serve; and Zoe just doesn't stay in position ... they're a mess," she commented under her breath.

"Cheer up, Mel," Cindy chirped one day after a close loss. "Your arm will be stronger before you know it! I am praying for your speedy recovery."

"I don't think even prayers will help me heal in time for this season, which means our chances of making the play-offs are pretty low," Mel replied.

Cindy looked surprised and hurt. Mel had shocked herself too. Logically she knew that it wasn't God's fault that she had been hurt, and usually she did turn to prayer during tough times. Now all she felt was numb—and angry! She wondered how she had become so bitter. Still, she couldn't shake it. She went to every game but was far from supportive; Mel's blues began to bring everyone down.

"This is the worst thing that could possibly happen to me, and I'm so angry," Mel blurted out to her parents one night. "What college coaches are going to look at me now? Junior year is so important ... I'm losing the most valuable time."

"The doctor said you are healing nicely, Mel, but it takes time," said Mel's mom. "Your best course of action is to put all your energy into the therapy so that you can really get back to your best shape. If you stay negative, it will slow down your progress."

Holding back tears, Mel stormed from the room and turned on the TV in hope of escape. As she flipped through the channels, she came across a segment about the US Women's Paralympic Sitting Volleyball Team. On the screen was a group of smiling women, some without legs, others with only one arm. But they were all playing the game they loved—with enthusiasm. Listening to each of these women's stories was humbling. When the segment finished, Mel sat quietly on the floor of her family room, letting it all sink in.

Speaking to herself, she said, "Wow! These women are amazing! They're great athletes and such supportive teammates. It's hard to believe that they made it so far facing so many obstacles—but they did, and they are smiling."

Over the next few days, Melanie replayed that segment in her mind and felt the hard ball of anger inside of her begin to melt. She felt moved to pray. "God, I am sorry for turning my back on You. Thank You for opening my eyes and heart through these incredible women athletes. Please help my arm heal and improve my attitude." As she prayed, feelings of shame, regret, humility, and, finally, joy flooded over her. Looking down at her cast in a new light, she said out loud, "At least I have my arm. It may not be working well right now, but it is healing and it's still a part of me, so I'm very lucky!"

"Mel, who are you talking to?" her mother asked as she came into the room.

"Just myself," Mel responded. "Mom, I saw this incredible story about handicapped women who play on the US Paralympic Sitting Volleyball Team. They actually play real volleyball without arms, legs, fingers—it's wild! But they are all so happy and nice to one another. It got me thinking about how poorly I've been handling my situation."

"Well, Mel, being disappointed is very human," said Mel's mom. "You love volleyball, and you happen to be very good at it. So it's been extremely hard to sit on the sidelines all season. That's understandable. Feeling a little sorry for yourself comes with the territory, but criticizing your teammates and lashing out at everyone in your path is not very becoming. I'm happy you are finally realizing that."

"I feel terrible, and I want to make it right," said Mel.

She picked up the phone and dialed Coach Rayburn.

"Coach, it's Mel. How come you haven't kicked me off the team for bad behavior?" she asked with a chuckle. "I mean, I'm glad you haven't, but my attitude has been so poor since I broke my arm, and tonight it really hit me, so … I'm sorry! And I promise that I'll be your biggest cheerleader and help however I can for the rest of the season—even with my arm in a cast!"

Coach Rayburn was delighted with Mel's turnaround and said, "That's the girl I had in mind for captain next year!"

One by one, Melanie dialed all her teammates to apologize and ask for their forgiveness.

"Cindy, I am so embarrassed by how poorly I've treated you lately. You're such a great friend and awesome teammate. I think your prayers are working, because the biggest thing that needed healing was my attitude, and I finally realized that. I don't know what came over me, but I can promise you that the nasty part of me is gone."

Cindy was pleased and very understanding—a true friend.

At practice the next day, the whole team seemed revitalized. Melanie's dark fog had lifted, and her new, thankful perspective infused the team with enthusiasm and resolve.

"Go Eagles! That's it, Jen—what a powerful serve! Way to go at the net, Amy!" Mel's voice grew hoarse from all her cheering, and the season ended on a happy note with the Eagles in third place.

START THE CONVERSATION

God, help me to be a good sport on and off the field. Help me to recognize and accept the role of sports in my life. If I can use my talents to bring Your message to others, please guide me and let Your will be done.

MORE GOOD NEWS: ECCLESIASTES 3:1–14

In these words we hear that our days and years, our comings and goings, are all in God's hands. We learn to trust and accept His master design for our lives.

FIRST STEP

Encourage your child to research famous athletes who have achieved balance and perspective by placing their trust in God. At a family dinner, have them share three motivating points they learned. Examples include David Robinson (NBA), Albert Pujols (MLB), Tim Tebow (NFL), Tamika Catchings (WNBA), Mariano Rivera (MLB), Joe Gibbs (NFL, NASCAR), Allyson Felix (track), Jeremy Lin (NBA), Gabby Douglas (gymnastics), and Zach Johnson (PGA).

Section II

Embrace the Rock

Once our children accept the truths found in section I, they will be ready to deepen their relationship with God the Father through His son, Jesus Christ. Their faith will be strengthened each time they embrace the rock (i.e., rely on the mercy, wisdom and love of Christ when dealing with nerves, ego, disappointments, teammates, and coaches).

"FOR THE LORD YOUR GOD IS GOING WITH
YOU!...AND HE WILL GIVE YOU VICTORY."

DEUTERONOMY 20:4

Anxiety

Don't worry about anything; instead, pray about everything. Tell God what you need, and thank him for all he has done. Then you will experience God's peace, which exceeds anything we can understand. His peace will guard your hearts and minds as you live in Christ Jesus.

—Philippians 4:6–7 NLT

There are many times when our children become stressed or anxious before or during competition. While nerves are a normal part of preparation, they can also become a debilitating obsession that saps the fun out of sports. When the disciples became anxious about Jesus's words at the last supper he told them, "Do not let your hearts be troubled. Trust in God; trust also in me" (John 14:1 NIV). This is a nice sentiment, but in order to trust in God and have faith in His love for them, our children need to *know* God and *believe* His message.

Through daily prayer, Bible reading, and quiet reflection, our children will realize that God has a plan for their lives. With this strong foundation of faith, they can approach any circumstance with peaceful confidence in the mercy and grace of God. We are reassured of this in Romans 8:31 (ESV): "If God is for us, who can be against us?" God is already on their side—in the batter's box, on the foul line, swimming laps in the pool, running on the track, standing on the balance beam—everywhere. He is their constant trusted companion.

In Mark 10:27 (ESV) we are told, "Jesus looked at them and said, with man it is impossible, but not with God; for all things are possible with God." Even though God is always with our children, He does not guarantee victory or success the way they may define it. It only assures our children that no matter the situation, if they glorify God by using the talents He gave them to the best of their ability, God will use all His power to bring about His will for them. The results may not always be what they want or understand, but knowing they come from a loving God should bring peace to their hearts.

When our children understand that all their abilities are blessings from God and that He is ultimately in control, it should become much easier for them to handle pressure situations with humility and confidence. Paul explains in 1 Peter 5:6–7 (NIV), "Humble yourselves, therefore, under God's mighty hand, that he may lift you up in due time. Cast all your anxiety on him because he cares for you." The greatest amount of practice is sometimes not enough to quell pregame jitters. By placing their hopes and anxieties in God's hands, our children will be prepared physically and spiritually to handle any circumstance. Joshua 1:9 (NIV) is a great pep talk: "Have I not commanded you? Be strong and courageous. Do not be terrified; do not be discouraged, for the Lord your God will be with you wherever you go." Sure, a few butterflies are natural before a big event, but they can be calmed with the knowledge that "by the grace of God, I am what I am."

RIPPLES FROM THE ROCK

Pete is a kid with a lot of talent who also deals with a lot of anxiety. When nerves start to get in the way of the game he loves, this ten-year-old boy has a big decision to make. "Inspired Decisions" highlights Pete's journey from getting physically ill in every game to a thoughtful decision that lightens his spirit and ultimately puts the game (and his life) back into perspective again. This is an important lesson for so many young athletes and their parents to learn together.

Inspired Decisions

Making the travel basketball team was a thrill for Pete, a typical ten-year-old boy who loved to play ball. He couldn't wait to get fitted for his uniform and hit the court for practice.

"This is a big commitment, Pete," his dad explained after the coach called to share the good news. "You'll be playing ball at a higher level against other really good players. You are certainly capable of it, and it will be a great experience. Just bring your love and passion for basketball with a willingness to listen and learn. Play with all your heart, and above all be a team player."

"I will, Dad!" Pete replied happily as he headed out to the driveway to practice.

Pete thought the first practice was fun. He liked being introduced to his teammates and hearing Coach Mike lay out the exciting season ahead. There would be practices two to three times per week and two games every weekend. Basketball bliss! Pete's dad was right; it was a big commitment. The two-hour practices were tough workouts as they conditioned and then went through countless drills. Some were fun, and others were boring, but he was learning a lot. Little by little, Coach Mike assigned kids to their positions.

"Pete, I like your shot and can see you are locked into the game, so I'd like to put you at small forward," Coach said one day.

"I can do that, Coach!" Pete replied, and he dedicated himself to being the best small forward who ever hit the fifth-grade travel circuit.

He was excited, but nervous too, anticipating their first game. During the weeks of practice, Pete realized that Coach could be kind of intense, and he found himself worried that he might disappoint him—or worse, make him mad.

Game day arrived. Pete felt good warming up and even better when Coach put him in the starting lineup. The sound of the ref's whistle put the ball in motion, and the game began.

"Move it! ... Pass the ball! ... Don't shoot! ... Bring it back out!" Pete's ears pounded with what sounded like angry shouts from Coach Mike. Combined with the parents' voices in the stands and the refs' loud whistles, Pete began to feel as if he were in another world. His stomach knotted, his eyes glazed over, and he no longer trusted his instincts. He froze on the court, turning the ball over time after time.

"Take him out!" Coach Mike yelled to his assistant, and Pete found himself bent over on the end of the bench, his nerves a jangled mess.

They eked out a win, but Coach Mike said they had played sloppily and he expected better from them next time. Pete left the game feeling low.

"Good first game, buddy," his mom chirped on the ride home.

"No it wasn't ... I stink!" Pete replied heatedly, tears stinging his eyes.

"Whoa … where is that attitude coming from?" his dad asked. "We were in the bleachers and watched you all play a tough game of basketball. Sure, there were some mistakes, but there were also a lot of great plays."

"Coach told us we were sloppy. Didn't you hear him yelling at me during the game?" Pete asked. "Then he finally took me out, and I sat on the bench the rest of the time."

"Well, he was calling out plays to everyone, son; I don't think he was singling you out from the team," his dad explained.

"I think he was mad, and some of my teammates agreed. We felt like he was yelling at us the whole game," Pete complained. "It made me very nervous, and I couldn't play my best game."

They drove the rest of the way home quietly, each thinking about the game and how to handle the situation. Later that night Pete's parents called him into the family room to talk about what had happened and to figure out a plan for dealing with Coach's game-day personality. With some rest and food under his belt, Pete found that his mood was happier and he wasn't as worried. They all agreed that it might have been a bad day for Coach Mike and decided to put the experience behind them.

"It's an important lesson, Pete, because throughout your life you will be dealing with all kinds of people in many different situations. Not everyone will have the same values as you do, so what they say and do may shock you. But if you have faith in God, you can stand strong in the most trying times. When you work hard and think of God as your coach, you'll always be a winner," his dad explained.

Pete continued to go to practices, improving his game along the way. Coach Mike seemed to be happy with what he was doing on the court, but weekend after weekend, the yelling during games continued; and try as he might, Pete could not shake the nerves that overcame him. He began to lose confidence and started worrying all the time. He'd break out into cold sweats or get severe headaches prior to the games. Suddenly he hated the game he used to love.

One night at dinner Pete blurted out, "I don't want to play travel anymore!"

When his parents asked why, he told them, "I don't feel like I'm as good as the other kids, and I just can't concentrate with all the yelling."

They discussed the pros and cons of quitting the team halfway through the season. Pete's parents believed in seeing a commitment through until the end; however, they were concerned for their son's mental and emotional health. In the end they decided that it would be a good idea to have a meeting with Coach Mike. Pete didn't like this idea; he was embarrassed to sit across from Coach Mike and admit that he made him nervous. But his parents said they would sit with him and help to explain the situation.

Coach Mike was very friendly and nice when they got to his house. Pete's dad started the conversation by saying how thrilled Pete was to be playing travel basketball and how much he had learned over the past months at practice.

"The problem is that Pete is having a difficult time handling the pressure of game day," his dad confided. "We respect you and appreciate the time you put in with the kids, Mike, but truthfully your game-day coaching style is unnerving for Pete. He takes your yelling and play-by-play calling out very personally, to the point where he begins to feel sick and freeze out on the court. He's been trying really hard to work through it, but he just cannot seem to shake those jitters, and he has lost his confidence, so he is considering stepping down from the team."

"Wow! I had no idea you were feeling this way, Pete. I guess now I understand why you've been freezing up during the games. I'm always surprised by that, because you are a good player."

"Uh, yeah, I guess I get kind of all jumbled up out there," Pete said shakily.

"Well, I have to admit that I don't think there is much I can do about my coaching style. After twenty years of doing this, I'm kind of stuck in my ways," Coach Mike chuckled. "But I'd really like you to stick with it, Pete; you have some potential."

He patted him on the back and then added, "Think about it, and remember—when I'm yelling, I'm not really mad at you; I'm just trying to bring the best out in the team."

"Okay, Coach, I'll think about it. Thanks." Pete shook his hand, and then he and his parents left.

On the ride home, Pete realized that it would be difficult to separate the Coach Mike in the living room from the Coach Mike on the court. Although he was flattered by the coach's encouragement, he knew continuing on the team would mean facing his anxieties.

Following his dad's advice, and with his parents' ongoing support, Pete did continue through the end of the travel season. He still dreaded game days, but he said a prayer before every game that God would take away his anxiety and help him tune out Coach Mike's yelling. Some days he still froze, but others, when he felt stronger, he made some nice plays and felt good about the sport again. At the award ceremony, Coach Mike said something nice about each player, and when it was Pete's turn, he told him he had the stuff good athletes are made of: instinct, a hard work ethic, and strength of character. He said that no matter what he decided to do in life, those characteristics would make him successful. Pete felt good about that and was glad he stayed with the team.

However, Pete has already told his parents that when next year comes around he may not try out for the travel team. What will happen between now and then, nobody but God knows. Pete is just planning to keep practicing and talking with God as he explores all the possibilities. He knows that when the time comes, God will lead him in the right direction.

START THE CONVERSATION

Jesus, may Your will be done as I try my very hardest at [fill in the sport]. Please take away my worries, and fill my heart with Your peace so my nerves don't take over the moment. Help my teammates do the same thing so that we are all relaxed and supportive of one another.

MORE GOOD NEWS: JEREMIAH, CHAPTER 1

In the story of young Jeremiah, we hear how God has great plans for each of us and that even if what He asks us to do seems difficult or frightening, He will always give us everything we need to see it through. The key is to listen to God and trust in His plans for our lives. He will do great things through each of us if we follow Him!

FIRST STEP

Have your child visualize something positive that happened to him or her in sports. In that mental image, suggest your child insert Jesus by his or her side, cheering him or her on or giving a high five. Now have your child visualize a disappointing moment in sports, and have him or her visualize Jesus by their side again, cheering him or her on or giving a big hug. Reinforce that Jesus is with your child always.

"LET THEM HAVE DOMINION OVER THE FISH"

GENESIS 1:26

Self-Confidence

God has said, "never will I leave you; never will I forsake you." So we say with confidence, "The Lord is my helper; I will not be afraid. What can man do to me?"

—Hebrews 13:5–6 NIV

Self-confidence is a key ingredient to success in sports and all areas of life. It is a strong belief in oneself and one's abilities. Some kids display a wealth of it, while others struggle to find it; yet with the proper insight, all young athletes should have a healthy level of self-confidence. True self-confidence, not to be confused with conceit, flows from confidence in God, who loves His children and gives them unique abilities. As their creator, He is also the ultimate coach, the one on whom all our children's hopes and worries should rest. In Jeremiah 17:7 (NLT), the Lord says, "Blessed are those who trust in the Lord and have made the Lord their hope and confidence."

Our children have been blessed with unique talents. Whether they are speedy runners, agile dribblers, powerhouse hitters, exuberant cheerleaders, strong leaders, or quick learners, their talents are gifts from God. The key to helping children develop their self-confidence is first to acknowledge that these gifts are given to them by God according to His divine plan, and then to work hard developing them in order to accomplish good things in God's name. In Genesis 21:22 (NAS) we read, "God is with you in all that you do." John tells us in 1 John 5:14 (NIV), "This is the confidence we have in approaching God: That if we ask anything according to his will, he hears us." These affirming verses remind our children to draw their confidence from the grace of God.

It is important to nurture self-confidence in a balanced way, keeping the relationship between God and child in perspective. At times, our children can get off track. Some young athletes become conceited when they forget to acknowledge the source of their talents and claim all the glory for themselves. Other children hide their talents because they are shy or insecure. Both can learn from Jesus's words in Matthew 5:14–16 (NAS): "You are the light of the world. A city set on a hill cannot be hidden; nor does anyone light a lamp and put it under a basket, but on a lampstand, and it gives light to all who are in the house. Let your light shine before men in such a way that they may see your good works, and glorify your Father who is in heaven."

God has all the power. Once our children develop a relationship with God and agree to follow His will for their lives, they can face any situation with courage and self-confidence. However, if they choose to rely solely on coaches, teammates, and trainers, without acknowledging God, they might encounter unmanageable issues that cause them strife and prevent them from fulfilling their true potential. Consider Psalm 146:3–4 (NIV): "Do not put your trust in princes, in mortal men, who cannot save. When their spirit departs, they return to the ground; on that very day their plans come to nothing." Also look to Psalm 118:8 (NAS): "It is better to take refuge in the Lord than to trust in man."

Our children may not always like or understand the ups and downs along their sports journey. It may be tempting for them to lose faith or fall back on human instincts when times are most frustrating. These are the testing situations that challenge them to grow in faith and rely on God's guidance. Jesus said in Matthew 17:20 (NIV), "I tell you the truth, if you have faith as small as a mustard seed you can say to this mountain, 'move from here to there' and it will move. Nothing will be impossible for you." When this approach becomes a habit, our children will become stronger, more confident athletes who are at peace with themselves and trusting of the bigger picture. This is underscored in Hebrews 10:35–36 (NAS) when Paul assures us, "Therefore, do not throw away your confidence, which has a great reward. For you have need of endurance, so that when you have done the will of God, you may receive what was promised." These words should be extremely comforting to our children and should give them a tremendous source of confidence, especially when they remember, "By the grace of God, I am what I am."

RIPPLES FROM THE ROCK

We all have moments when our confidence fails us. Young athletes are especially prone to nerves when they face what seem to be insurmountable odds. Even though they have proven themselves to be very capable in their sport, it is easy for them to second-guess their abilities when a big game or event is on the line. These are the times when it takes more than muscle; it takes a combination of spirit, mind, body, and heart to help them take the risk and endure the experience. In the story "Play-Offs," we find good insights into this issue, which is common among young athletes.

Play-Offs

"Yes!" Jack shouted, high-fiving his teammates as they ran off the field following their season-ending victory. "We are off to Willow Park for the play-offs!" He grinned as Dave squirted water over his head. "After all these years, we are getting our chance. We'll show them!"

During practice before the play-offs, Coach Ron made a big announcement—game one would be against the first-seeded Ravens team. Everyone knew this team was dominant. They had steamrolled through the regular season with the most potent lineup anyone could remember. Taking the mound for the Admirals would be their ace pitcher, Jack Duggan.

As Jack walked home after practice, he was crestfallen. He had won many games for the Admirals during the season and was proud to be their most reliable pitcher. But he knew there was no way he could pitch his team to victory against the big-hitting Ravens. His mind played images of a blowout game with batter after Ravens batter cracking his pitches over the fence.

"Hey, Jack," a familiar voice called out, bringing him back to earth.

Jack turned around to see Pastor Jim from the local church he attended with his family each week. PJ, as most people called Pastor Jim, was a big fan of baseball and asked Jack when he was playing next.

"Oh, hi PJ," Jack said, walking closer to him.

"You look like a boy who has the weight of the world on his shoulders," PJ observed. "What's going on?"

"Well, we just found out that our first game will be against the Ravens. You know how good they are. I'm afraid my pitching isn't strong enough," said Jack.

"That doesn't sound like the Jack I know. Where's your self-confidence? Seems to me you had a pretty good record this season too."

Jack smiled. "I guess you're right. It's just that I waited so long to get to the play-offs and would rather start off with an easier team."

"Obviously this is where God wants you to be. Why don't you think about it this way—you are playing for God. He gave you that powerful arm, and He wants you to use it to the best of your ability against the Ravens. When you're on the mound and feeling nervous, remember the Holy Spirit is right there with you, giving you all the strength and courage you need."

"Will God help me strike out the Ravens?" Jack asked enthusiastically.

"God alone knows the answer," PJ replied. "But He will provide everything you need to get through the game—win or lose. That is His promise. And He doesn't want you to give up before you even hit the field."

Jack still had plenty of pregame butterflies when the big day arrived, but he took the mound feeling confident that he was where God wanted him to be. He looked out in the stands and saw PJ and his parents smiling at him. The game was scoreless through five innings, and Jack was pitching masterfully. He gave up a few hits, but no runs crossed home plate. Finally, in the bottom of the sixth and final inning, with two outs and no one on base, the Ravens' best hitter smashed a ball just over the left field wall for a walk-off home run. The Admirals' season was over. Before Jack could even react to the sudden end of such a close game, the Ravens coach shook his hand and told him that was the best pitching performance he had ever seen from a sixth grader, and that he was extremely impressed with Jack's composure on the mound.

As Jack talked with PJ after the game, he expressed his disappointment at losing but said he was excited to have held the mighty Ravens scoreless for five innings.

"God wanted the Ravens to move on," he said. "They deserve it. They really are good. But you know, God gave me a great victory today also. I hung in there with the best team in the area for five innings."

PJ smiled and encouraged Jack to approach all things in life just as he did this baseball game—with confidence in the power of God.

START THE CONVERSATION

Dear Lord, fill me with Your spirit so that I may grow closer to You each day. Strengthen my faith so that I might have complete trust in You. Guide me along the many roads I will travel. Help me to understand that Your love for me should be the true source of my confidence and that together we can face any circumstance.

MORE GOOD NEWS: 1 SAMUEL 17:1–54

"Good things come in small packages" is an appropriate way to describe the story of David and Goliath. Compared to the massive, battle-tested Philistine Goliath, David is a small and inexperienced boy. But armed with God's blessings, David is confident that he can overcome insurmountable odds to defeat Goliath and lead the Israelites to victory.

FIRST STEP

Have your child try something he or she is a little nervous about. Perhaps playing a different position or facing tougher competition. Find something that challenges your child's comfort zone. Encourage him or her to trust in the Lord and follow through no matter the result. Then have your child share the feelings he or she had through every stage. Or have your child wear a blindfold for part of the day, doing all his or her usual activities without being able to see. Have him or her rely solely on prayer to accomplish his or her tasks. Encourage your child to picture God leading him or her in whatever he or she is doing. Have your child share his or her feelings about trusting God at the end of the experiment.

"HE WHO HAS BEEN STEALING MUST STEAL NO LONGER"

EPHESIANS 4:28

Pride / Humility

This is what the Lord says: "Don't let the wise boast in their wisdom, or the powerful boast in their power ... But those who wish to boast should boast in this alone: that they truly know me and understand that I am the Lord who demonstrates unfailing love and who brings justice and righteousness to the earth, and that I delight in these things."

—Jeremiah 9:23–24 NLT

We have all encountered "natural" athletes. Born to play, they are light years ahead of their peers in raw talent and athleticism. From an early age, they seem to perform with effortless success. They may even have a certain local celebrity status in school or around town. In the small world of a child, these conditions may eventually lead to feelings of pride. They forget their talents are from God and begin to take personal credit for their performances. Even those young athletes who put in extra practice to make up for their apparent lack of natural ability can fall into the trap of ignoring God's role and believing their success is a result of personal effort alone. They start to believe their athletic accomplishments are indicative of a superior nature placing them above other kids their own age. This can lead our children down a path of bullying, forming exclusionary cliques, exercising rude and disrespectful behavior, and other poor character traits that ultimately dishonor God and any athletic blessings He has given them. We are warned in Proverbs to guard against this temptation. "When pride comes, then comes dishonor" (Proverbs 11:2 NAS). "Pride goes before destruction, and a haughty spirit before stumbling" (Proverbs 16:18 NAS). With each success, our children can feel more invincible. They may begin to squeeze out God as they bask in their own glory. Their prayer and Bible study start to take a backseat to pride. When this happens, it is important for our children to reorient their focus to the true source of their success. One Sabbath as Jesus ate in the house of a prominent Pharisee he told the guests, "For everyone who exalts himself will be humbled, and he who humbles himself will be exalted" (Luke 14:11 NAS).

Marginalizing their relationship with God will only lead to disappointment for our children. As discussed in the previous section, self-confidence is important, but when it is not rooted in confidence in God, it can lead to pride. When a young athlete excels at his or her sport and receives the recognition that goes with it, they can be tempted into thinking that they control their own destiny. But how many so-called prodigies wind up disillusioned when their peers catch up and offer more competition? How lost children can become when they define themselves solely by their athletic prowess and then suffer an injury that limits their ability to compete effectively. When children do not have a firm understanding of God's role in their lives, these can be truly difficult circumstances.

God made all children in His image, and He loves them unconditionally. It is only when our children accept this truth and put God at the center of their lives that they can claim success no matter the circumstances or outcome. We are told in Acts 20:24 (NIV), "I consider my life worth nothing to me, if only I may finish the race and complete the task the Lord Jesus has given me—the task of testifying to the gospel of God's grace." That is what our children are doing when they have success—testifying to the grace of God. It is the power and goodness of God manifested in them that should be recognized and celebrated. Romans 9:17 (ESV) says, "For this very purpose I have raised you up, that I might show my power in you." With this in mind, when our children get the winning basket, last-second goal, or walk-off hit, they should reflect on God's blessings and how He is working through them.

Knowing that God is in control and giving Him all the glory makes it much easier for our young athletes to remain humble and well balanced. We are told in James 4:6 (NIV), "God opposes the proud but gives grace to the humble." They will need that grace to handle the inevitable ups and downs intrinsic to sports. If young athletes accept their triumphs as gifts from God, they will be better able to accept difficult moments as also part of His plan. In Mark 9:33–35 (NAS), we read the story of Jesus talking to His disciples and explaining what it really means to be the greatest: "He began to question them, 'What were you discussing on the way?' but they kept silent, for on the way they had discussed with one another which of them was the greatest. Sitting down He called the twelve and said to them 'If anyone wants to be first, he shall be last of all and servant of all.'" Our children need to learn to put God first. They should acknowledge that His will is at work in their lives and the lives of their peers. This will help them to realize that any victories or defeats are not theirs personally but are part of God's overall plan. That is why it is so important to accept "By the grace of God, I am what I am."

RIPPLES FROM THE ROCK

Sometimes success and notoriety sneak up on children, and the alluring effects of these things can lead them down a path they never imagined. New people and opportunities appear, and without giving things much thought, they make choices that are most likely out of character but put them in an exciting light. These decisions are not without lasting repercussions, as Mark discovers in the story "Life in the (Fri)End Zone."

Life in the (Fri)End Zone

Mark, Freddie, Ian, and Stan had been best friends since kindergarten. Growing up in the same neighborhood, they spent school day afternoons and summers hanging out together, usually playing ball. They'd raid one another's garages for tennis balls, basketballs, baseballs, bats, racquets, and hit the local streets, courts, or fields for action. Wherever they went and whatever they did, these four boys were together. Every year, they played on the same teams, sharing the victories and defeats that come with competitive sports.

The summer before their freshman year of high school, the foursome was tighter than ever, attending special camps and going to the gym together to get ready for football tryouts. Making the high school team was a big deal, and like everything they'd done before, they planned to do it together. There was a lot of competition, though, since three area middle schools fed into the high school. So they worked hard and cheered one another along. After a week of strenuous, stressful tryouts, they returned to the neighborhood, hanging out and waiting to hear from the coach.

By Sunday, each of the boys got a call. It was good news, in that they had all made the team, but one of the calls was different—Mark had actually been put on junior varsity. They were all pumped up and happy for one another, yet it felt strange to know that Mark would not be with the rest of the gang on the freshman team.

During the hot month of August, they practiced every day, conditioning and learning basic team strategies. Every night, the boys walked home together, like old times. Mark said the older guys were pretty cool, but he missed being on the same team with his friends. They all agreed to stay tight no matter what. Then the season started. The freshman team played pretty well, but the JV team was unstoppable. As the games unfolded, Mark emerged as a key running back. He was featured in many game plays, highlighted in the local press, and became the coaches' go-to guy. His friends were really happy for him. But with each passing week, Mark seemed harder to reach. Suddenly he started hanging out with his older teammates and began dating one of the cheerleaders. Whenever the guys did get together in the neighborhood, Mark only wanted to talk about himself and the latest JV victory, reliving his amazing plays. By Thanksgiving, the foursome was minus one—Mark. Freddie, Stan, and Ian were actually angry with him and admitted to one another that Mark had changed—and not for the better. It got so bad that they avoided him in the neighborhood and ignored him at school. He didn't seem to notice or care, though, because he was so wrapped up with his new group.

When football ended and the glow of the stadium lights faded, Mark didn't feel as connected to the team as he previously had. They were sophomores and juniors, off to other activities and parties that didn't seem to include him anymore. He started to feel out of place, as if he didn't have an identity without football. For the first time in a while he thought of his old buddies and realized he missed them, but when he tried to reconnect with them, he got a cool reception.

One day he approached them at lunch and said, "What's up with you guys?"

Freddie, Stan, and Ian looked at one another and back at Mark.

"We should be asking you that question," replied Ian.

Mark just gave them a strange look and shrugged.

"Listen, man, the truth is you changed over these last few months. Popularity got to your head, and you did something we all promised one another we'd never do—you ditched us," said Freddie.

"Yeah, it's like we weren't cool enough anymore and you were all caught up with your new friends," added Stan.

With that, they got up and walked away.

Mark was shocked, but as he thought about it during the rest of the day, he realized that they were right. That night he spoke with his parents about it, asking for their advice.

"We were very excited about you playing JV, Mark, and we are very proud of your accomplishments," his mom said, "but with privilege comes responsibility."

His father continued. "When it comes down to it, son, your talents are a gift from God and should be used to glorify Him, not you. Popularity is appealing, but as you can see, it's not lasting. Friendship, on the other hand, is forever—if you keep nurturing it."

Mark let this all sink in. First he felt really embarrassed for his bad attitude, and then he was worried that he would never regain the trust of his best friends.

After sleeping—and praying—on the situation, Mark had an idea. He texted Stan, Freddie, and Ian, asking them to meet him at his house after school that day. When three o'clock came, his friends were on his front lawn, acting very cool. Things still seemed tense.

He passed around a plate of his mom's famous chocolate-marshmallow cookies to break the ice, and while they were chewing, Mark said, "You guys are so right ... I have been a terrible friend! We promised to stick together, and I let my ego take over. I am really sorry! I've been thinking about it and ... no matter how awesome it was to star in those games and get some attention, I would trade it all to have you guys back as my best friends!"

Freddie, Ian, and Stan looked at one another, shrugged, and smiled.

"I guess everyone messes up at times," Freddie said.

"Yeah, man, we're not all perfect," Ian chimed in.

"And as long as you finally realized what's really important—that being us"—Stan nudged Mark and laughed—"we forgive you. Just don't let it happen again!"

They cleared the air, and over the next few months Mark showed that he was worthy of their renewed friendship. Little by little the foursome came back together again, and by summer they were hanging out by the park, shooting hoops, picking up baseball games, and raiding one another's refrigerators and garages. Mark's experience made him realize that sometimes God puts good friends in your life to keep you humble and help you see the true source of your talent.

START THE CONVERSATION

Have your child make up his or her own prayer to say before every practice and game. It can be very simple. For example, "Thank You, God, for giving me the ability to _____. Thank You also for making it possible for me to play _____, a sport I truly love. Please help me do my best, and watch over all my teammates and coaches."

MORE GOOD NEWS: DANIEL, CHAPTER 4

What happens when a man proclaims himself better than all others? King Nebuchadnezzar finds out when a dream he has about being thrown into the wild with all the animals comes true. He spends seven years stripped of his kingship, wandering and eating with the animals until he accepts the fact that the Lord is sovereign over all. At the end of the seven years, Nebuchadnezzar is restored to power and becomes an enlightened king because he recognizes the one true Lord God.

FIRST STEP

Ask your child to identify three to five kids his or her age whose athletic skills he or she admires. Have your child name the particular skills and encourage him or her to tell these players he or she admires their talents. Also have your child identify talents God has blessed him or her with, and encourage him or her to thank God daily for these gifts.

"NOT A SINGLE ONE OF THEM WILL BE ABLE TO STAND UP AGAINST YOU."

JOSHUA 10:8

Disappointment

And the Lord said to me, "My grace is sufficient for you, for power is perfected in weakness." Most gladly, therefore, I will rather boast about my weaknesses, so that the power of Christ may dwell in me. Therefore I am well content with weaknesses, with insults, with distresses, with persecutions, with difficulties, for Christ's sake; for when I am weak, then I am strong."

—2 Corinthians 12:9–10 NAS

Youth sports can be filled with bitter disappointments, and no one who competes is exempt from some heartache now and then. A bad game, a costly error, missing the winning shot, striking out with the bases loaded, dropping a touchdown pass, not making a team, or any of the other myriad reasons our children can despair are unavoidable occurrences at one time or another. Sports can be extremely important to children. Learning to accept that things don't always go as they planned will help them develop a more stable mental attitude and will provide valuable lessons in sports and beyond.

The important thing to remember is that God is in charge and He has a plan. Paul tells us in Romans 8:28 (NIV), "And we know that in all things God works for the good of those who love Him." We may not fully understand why things happen, but if we stay faithful to God, we can be assured the reasons will be revealed in time. When things go wrong, our children need only turn to God with open hearts, seeking to do His will. God is not keeping a scorecard based on strikeouts, fumbles, air balls or losses. He wants our children to grow stronger through hardships and to develop inner strength. We are encouraged in Hebrews 10:35–36 (NAS): "Therefore, do not throw away your confidence, which has a great reward. For you have need of endurance, so that when you have done the will of God, you may receive what was promised."

It can be difficult for our children to suffer through hardships, but accepting that God's plan for them is unfolding will make these trying moments easier to endure. He knows best what our children need for today and their future. In James 1:2–4 (NIV) we are told, "Consider it pure joy, my brothers, whenever you face trials of any kind, because you know that the testing of your faith develops perseverance. Perseverance must finish its work so that you may be mature and complete, not lacking anything." Our children need to accept the inevitable disappointments as part of God's master plan. It certainly will not be fun or easy but trusting in God through difficult times, and accepting His will for their lives is another way to glorify God. Paul assures us, "Therefore we do not lose heart. Though outwardly we are wasting away, yet inwardly we are being renewed day by day. For our light and momentary troubles are achieving for us an eternal glory that far outweighs them all" (2 Corinthians 4:16–17 NIV).

By keeping their attitudes and tempers in check when disappointments come their way, our children can be wonderful witnesses to other athletes. For truly, with God on their team it is always a winning situation. Although they may find this hard to do all the time, the more they practice, the easier it will be as they keep in mind "By the grace of God, I am what I am."

RIPPLES FROM THE ROCK

In a society where children are praised for every little accomplishment, it can be difficult for them to accept just being ordinary when competing in youth sports. Despite the frustrations that may originally arise from them, occasional disappointments, when viewed with the right attitude, can reveal great opportunities. Find out what happens to Nancy in the eye-opening story "Why 'Me' Became 'We.'"

Why "Me" Became "We"

Growing up on Franklin Court was a soccer player's dream. Two sets of old garbage cans served as makeshift goals at the end of the cul-de-sac. There were plenty of kids in the neighborhood, and someone always had a ball, so afternoon and weekend games were a way of life for Nancy Dowd. Even on days when neighborhood games weren't played, she could be found in her yard, working on her moves. Nancy started practicing and playing these pickup games almost from the moment she could walk.

Mrs. Olsen once remarked, "I have never seen anyone that young bounce a ball on their knee so easily."

Another neighbor, Mr. Blanco, would see her racing toward the end of their road and tell his wife, "That Nancy Dowd has got to be the fastest little girl in town."

Nancy developed quite an impressive reputation on Franklin Court.

Summer was over, school was in session, and on this particular day Nancy was extremely excited. She was finally on an official seven-year-old soccer team, and today was the first practice.

"I can't wait to show the coach all my moves," she gushed to her mother. "Wait until the other girls see what I can do."

"Whoa! Slow down, Nancy," her mom said. "Don't get too far ahead of yourself. This is your first experience with organized soccer, so just relax and have fun."

"I will, Mom," Nancy shot back as she flew out the door. "But just wait and see; I'm going to be really good."

Mrs. Dowd just chuckled and rolled her eyes.

Down at the field, Coach DeSalvo was very friendly as he explained his plan for the season. "I want all of you to become better soccer players, so we will spend a lot of time on dribbling and control drills at practice. We will also do quite a bit of conditioning. The only thing I ask is that you listen and try your best. Other than that—let's have fun!"

During the first practice, Nancy realized that she was not the fastest girl on the team, but she could keep up with them. As the days passed, Nancy learned her drills and worked hard at practice. She was excited to play in the first game. One afternoon following practice, the coach brought the girls together to talk about his plan for opening day. As he called out the starting lineup, Nancy's heart pounded with anticipation. However, she did not hear her name.

She felt deflated. *I'm going to be nothing more than a sub, a benchwarmer,* she thought to herself. *Did I do something wrong? I think I am just as good as the starters.*

At dinner that night, Nancy was not very pleasant company.

"What's bothering you, sugar plum?" her dad asked.

"Nothing." She pouted, pushing the food around on her plate.

"How did practice go today?" he said.

Suddenly Nancy burst into tears. "I am not starting this Sunday's game," she sobbed, putting her head on the table. "I don't know why; Coach just didn't put me in as a starter. I worked so hard for nothing."

Nancy's parents exchanged a look, then asked her to come sit with them on the couch.

"Honey, we know things are not going exactly as you planned, but let's take a look at the situation. You are playing the sport you love. You are learning a lot and improving with every practice. You also have a great coach and nice teammates," her mom said.

"But I've always been so good, so fast. You know what the neighbors say," Nancy complained.

"Yes, you have natural talent for soccer, and that is a gift. But it doesn't make you an automatic starter, particularly at seven years old. You still have to work hard to learn the plays, accept the coach's instruction and feedback, and become a team player. All this takes time, experience, and, most important, a positive attitude," her dad said.

Nancy listened and nodded in agreement. Kneeling down together to pray, Nancy and her parents thanked God for her chance to play on the soccer team. They asked God to help Nancy deal with her disappointments and grow from her experiences. They also prayed for Coach DeSalvo and her teammates.

Nancy kept these prayers going and over the next few weeks developed a brand-new attitude. "Hey, Mom, let me show you the cool move Joyce taught me at practice today," she said enthusiastically. "I can't believe how much I am learning; this is so much fun!"

As the season went on, Nancy began to realize that what had initially seemed to be a disappointment was actually a fantastic opportunity. She was learning a lot more about soccer at practices and by observing the girls from the bench. She made the most out of her limited playing time in games. With God's special graces, Nancy was able to keep a positive attitude even though things didn't always go as she planned. Now she knew what it meant to be part of a team and was able to appreciate the special talents each girl brought to the game. Once she noticed the bigger picture and accepted her role in it, she was able to relax, improve her soccer skills, and make new friends from all around town.

START THE CONVERSATION

Lift up my spirit, Lord, and help me find the good and see Your blessings even when it seems so hard to do.

MORE GOOD NEWS: LUKE 24:13–36

When we walk by sight alone, we often miss some of God's greatest blessings. In this gospel story, two of Jesus's followers walk despondently to Emmaus lamenting Jesus's death and worrying about what is to come. Their promised savior has just been crucified, and it seems all their hopes and dreams have been snatched away. A stranger joins them on their journey and begins to enlighten them on the meaning of the scriptures. They begin to realize that the disappointment they felt was due to their lack of understanding God's plan. Their eyes are soon opened, and the disappointment is replaced with the joy and the promise of God's love through His son, Jesus.

FIRST STEP

Choose a movie or book with a challenging, thought-provoking theme. (*Facing the Giants* and *The Perfect Game* are two inspiring family movies, as a suggestion.) Watch or read it with your child, and then ask your child to make note of hardships, failures, and challenges the characters face. At the end have a discussion about these situations and the ways the characters overcame them. Another possible activity is to suggest that your child keep a journal to share his or her highlights and disappointments in regard to sports and life in general. Encourage your child to record these experiences while keeping his or her mind open to how they can learn from them.

"Accept instruction from his mouth and lay up"

Job 22:22 (NIV)

Teamwork

Because of the privilege and authority God has given me, I give each of you this warning: Don't think you are better than you really are. Be honest in your evaluation of yourselves, measuring yourselves by the faith God has given us. Just as our bodies have many parts and each part has a special function, so it is with Christ's body. We are many parts of one body, and we all belong to each other. In his grace, God has given us different gifts for doing certain things well.

—Romans 12:3–6 NLT

Teamwork is at the heart of every sport. It requires commitment, dedication, recognition of others, and putting aside ego and differences for the sake of a common goal. Becoming part of a team can be a life-changing experience for young athletes. They will be challenged to think outside of themselves and to accept that they are not in control. This is where God, the ultimate coach, comes in. He has a game plan for His young athletes, a divine reason for placing each and every person in his or her life. In Proverbs 27:17 (NIV) we are told, "As iron sharpens iron so one man sharpens another."

God wants our children to work together to build a team united in doing His will on earth. He wants them to be loving, supportive teammates under all circumstances. If a child is put on a team that is not his or her first choice, that child should stick it out and discover God's plan for him or her in that situation instead of complaining. By modeling patience and acceptance and having a Christ-centered attitude about team placements and new situations, our children can have a positive impact on a whole team.

Teamwork has a lasting impact on our children's lives. One young athlete may make a lifelong impression on another that isn't revealed until years later. A simple word of encouragement when a teammate is on the verge of giving up can make a big difference in that player's life. Our children can demonstrate godly character by staying positive and keeping faith in His divine plan even during their struggles. Dealing with success can be just as powerful a lesson. Praising God and acknowledging the role He plays in their lives shows teammates the value our children place on their relationship with God. While it may take place in the arena of sports instead of a church, this witness can encourage teammates to seek out a personal relationship with God through His son, Jesus, which will be a blessing through the course of their lifetime. It is important, therefore, for our children to trust that they are where God wants them to be at any given moment. Their words and actions will be a witness to God's love and compassion.

God may use our children as beacons of His love and grace to bring others closer to Him, or He may use others to teach our children a valuable lesson. For this reason, it is important to be open to every team experience.

In Romans 15:7 (NLT) Paul instructs, "Therefore, accept each other just as Christ has accepted you so that God will be given glory." Galatians 5:26 (ESV) similarly states, "Let us not become conceited, provoking one another, envying one another." Just as God accepts our children with all their mistakes, errors, penalties, fouls, and shortcomings, so should our children display godly character in dealing with their teammates and opponents. Regardless of how God decides to spread the talent among the team and around the league, our children should treat everyone with dignity and as one of His children. Even if they do not receive the respect they deserve, our children can be great witnesses of Christian living by turning the other cheek and accepting God's love as their reward.

In Hebrews 10:24 (NLT) Paul says, "Let us think of ways to motivate one another to acts of love and good works." Our children don't have to be stars of a team to demonstrate the light of Christ. They can be leaders by showing their teammates how to win with humility and lose with dignity. In Philippians 2:3–4 (NLT) Paul tell us, "Don't be selfish; don't try to impress others. Be humble, thinking of others as better than yourselves. Don't look out only for your own interests, but take an interest in others, too." It is so important for our children to be sensitive to the feelings and needs of others on their team. Games will come and go. Seasons will pass away. But relationships are part of life's journey. They will have many opportunities to touch others with God's love. Sports teams are no different. They can be great incubators for our children to learn how to put into practice the lessons Christ teaches them in the Bible.

If your child is having difficulties with teammates or coaching decisions, encourage him or her to stay faithful to God and be the best teammate he or she can be. Remind your child that God is the head coach and to keep their eyes on what wonderful things will come from His vision. Knowledge that all things come from God, including athletic ability, will keep our children's hearts in the right place and make them good teammates. It all starts by accepting the truth "By the grace of God, I am what I am."

RIPPLES FROM THE ROCK

In the story "Finding Victory in Defeat," a group of eleven- and twelve-year-old girls become shining examples of God's message on and off the basketball court. Contrary to so many stories of girls being mean to one another, this story is a testimony to the importance and power of teamwork.

Finding Victory in Defeat

These girls aren't very good at all, Diane thought as she dribbled the ball upcourt during practice. She was new to the eighth grade at St. Tims and had come from a championship basketball team in her old town. *This is going to be a tough season.*

The first game was a blowout. Diane darted all over the court, stealing, shooting, and calling out orders to her teammates, but she couldn't carry the game alone. The loss hit her hard.

At the next practice, Coach Johnson called the girls to midcourt to talk about the game. "Girls, you played hard, and I appreciate your efforts. We have to work on our defense and protect the ball a little bit more on offense. Diane, you were awesome. Be careful not to overdo it, though; you need to save your energy for the rest of the season," he said.

Diane was conflicted. These girls were so nice and had made her feel welcome at school. Yet she felt like the only one on the team who really cared about winning, and it made her impatient.

"Oh, come on!" Diane lashed out when Emily missed a hard pass during a game. "Tammy, you have to make that layup!" she muttered another time. She was embarrassed to be on the team.

The season went on, and despite Diane's Herculean efforts, the team kept losing games. Some were closer than others, but their record was still 0–10, and she was a wreck.

One day Coach Johnson asked her to stay after practice. She stood at the foul line, sinking shot after shot as they bantered about the UConn women's team.

"You're good enough to play for them one day," Coach Johnson said.

"Well, I don't know about that, but I'd love the chance," Diane replied.

"I guess it's hard for you to have such ability and be playing on a losing team," Coach said.

Not sure how to respond, Diane muttered, "Kinda."

"I get it, Diane. It's hard to come from a championship team to an 0 and 10 team. Truthfully, though, this is the best team I've ever coached," he said.

"Really?" Diane asked with a funny look on her face.

"Definitely! You know why? They have heart and know what it means to be good teammates. They support one another and stay up for every game even though they keep losing. I've learned so much from them. I don't like losing any more than you do, but I've started to realize that there are many ways to win. In my mind, these girls are all winners," Coach said.

Diane was speechless. Coach asked her to think about what he said and thanked her for adding her talents to the team. During the next few practices, she observed her teammates as they encouraged one another through difficult drills and praised one another for small accomplishments.

She realized that basketball didn't come easily for most of them but they were fully committed to giving it their very best. Diane's attitude about winning began to change slowly. Instead of trying to win games by herself, she started to get her teammates more involved by passing them the ball and encouraging them to shoot. She got excited at their small achievements and felt herself become absorbed in the chemistry of the team.

Before too long, the time came for the final game of the season. Mary stood at the foul line and dribbled the basketball nervously.

"Knock it down, Mary!" yelled Emily from the bench.

"Take a deep breath and bend your knees," Coach Johnson instructed.

With only five seconds left in the Rams' first-round play-off game, all eyes were on Mary. She could feel the pressure mount as the roaring crowd grew silent. Taking a deep breath to calm herself, Mary launched the ball into the air and watched it swish through the net.

"Way to go, Mary!" screamed Brittany.

"I knew you would do it!" Kathryn cheered as she high-fived Mary.

The rest of the team swarmed around Mary, celebrating and patting her on the back, while the opposing team took the ball out of bounds and ran out the clock. The game was over, and the Rams had lost—again. But that did nothing to dampen their enthusiasm.

The bus ride back to school after a 0–14 season could have been heartrending, but for this group of inspiring young women it was heartwarming. Coach Johnson beamed watching the girls jump around as if they had just won the championship instead of ending their season with another lopsided loss. Diane was in the middle of them all, laughing and looking every bit a winner. Somewhere along the road, these girls had stopped worrying about the scoreboard and accepted God's plan for their season. Although they were overmatched in nearly every game, they never exhibited any finger-pointing or hard feelings. These girls played with their hearts, experiencing individual and team milestones along the way, which drove them to work harder, cheer louder, and gain more respect for one another, on and off the court.

As a team, they had accomplished so much. It took fourteen games, but Mary had just made her first ever foul shot, and her teammates were so proud of her.

"Tammy, remember the time you stole the ball and drove the length of the court, ending with a sweet crossover and layup?" Mary asked her friend.

"I don't know," Tammy replied, blushing. "I think Kaitlin's three-pointer was the best shot of the season."

"What do you mean?" Kaitlin laughed. "I had my eyes closed, so that shot was pure luck."

"Never mind all this offense talk," Erin teased. "Did you guys see how aggressive I got rebounding over the last few games?"

This banter kept up the whole ride home as the girls relished the pure joy that comes from accepting God's will.

When the bus arrived back at school, Coach Johnson asked all the girls to sign a basketball for him.

"Tomorrow morning I am placing this basketball in the trophy case that stands in the school lobby," he told them. "I have coached three championship teams at this school. They were tough teams. The girls were not only quick and athletic but also had a very physical style of play. Your team ball will sit right alongside theirs."

Coach Johnson's voice began to quiver as tears came to his eyes. "No matter what the record shows, you girls are every bit the champions these previous teams were. It was truly a privilege to coach such a remarkable group of young ladies who played with such incredible heart. I am overwhelmed with pride for all that you accomplished this year."

Coach Johnson was not alone in his admiration for the team. At the league banquet a month later, coach after coach remarked on the impressive way the Rams supported one another through an otherwise tough season.

As the league president presented the Sportsmanship Award to the entire Rams team, she remarked, "You girls have shown many of the adults in this room, including parents and coaches from every team, what youth sports are all about. You didn't let the scoreboard decide whether or not you were winning the game. You stayed together and kept working hard. I have no doubt the results of this season and your outstanding attitude will benefit you in the years to come, both on and off the court."

"I couldn't agree more," Diane said to herself, smiling.

As the celebration neared an end, Coach Johnson gathered the girls, and their trophy, for one last team picture.

Next year many of them will be heading in different directions as they go off to high school, but they will always cherish their "perfect" 0–14 season.

START THE CONVERSATION

Have your child keep the team in prayer all season, asking God to keep them close and to help all the members realize their unique abilities and encourage each other in all situations.

MORE GOOD NEWS: NEHEMIAH 2:17–6:15

A group of neighbors committed to work together rebuilding the wall of Jerusalem despite being mocked and having obstacles placed in their way. They remained true to their goal, and each concentrated on a different section of the project. After fifty-two days, the wall was complete, much to the surprise of their enemies. Through teamwork, God's will is fulfilled by His faithful servants.

FIRST STEP

At the beginning of the season, host an informal event, such as a pizza party, where the players can relax and get to know one another. This will help build camaraderie on the team.

Section III

Treasure the Rock

Learning to tap into their inner rock and embracing the philosophies that support this lifestyle will lead our children to the ultimate treasure, which is joy and contentment in the presence of God. By letting go of earthly issues, they will feel a sense of freedom and find themselves participating in sports on a completely different level. They will play with a passion that comes from a deeper understanding and appreciation of the gifts God has given them.

"AFTER MUCH THOUGHT, I DECIDED
TO CHEER MYSELF."

ECCLESIASTES 2:3

Contentment

These things I have spoken to you, so that in Me you may have peace. In this world you will have tribulation, but take courage; I have overcome the world.

—John 16:33 NAS

Contentment is being at peace; it is an acceptance that you are where God wants you to be. Unfortunately, finding contentment in the supercharged environment of youth sports can be challenging. However, it is not impossible if our children draw on their inner rock, recognizing the special gifts God has given them and remembering they are part of His divine plan. Comparing themselves to others, lamenting about their shortcomings, or complaining about missed opportunities will never lead our children to the peace and happiness that God desires for them. They should recall each day how much God loves them and is there to help them along their life journey. Jeremiah 29:11 (NIV) emphasizes this awesome fact: "'For I know the plans I have for you', declares the Lord, 'plans to prosper you and not to harm you, plans to give you hope and a future."

When our children are playing for God, everything else will fall into place and they will feel content. By making the most of every situation, they glorify God. Paul tells us in 1 Corinthians 7:24 (NIV), "Brothers, each man, as responsible to God, should remain in the situation God called him to." It is important for young athletes to let go of envy and jealousy and to guard against impatience and frustration when things aren't going according to their schedule. We need to remind them that God's plan is at work and that all their experiences are part of it. He is also placing certain people (coaches, teammates, etc.) in their lives for a purpose. In Hebrews 13:5–6 (NLT) we are told, "Be satisfied with what you have. For God has said, 'I will never fail you. I will never abandon you.' So we can say with confidence, 'The Lord is my helper, so I will have no fear. What can mere people do to me?'"

There are many false role models in this world, and our children are constantly bombarded by these people and images. As early as possible, we as parents should teach them to tune out these loud, unruly false idols and tune into God. They can find true peace and contentment only by putting their lives in God's hands. God alone is all-loving and all-powerful. "I have learned the secret of being content in any and every situation ... I can do everything through Him who gives me strength" (Philippians 4:12–13 NIV). How comforting! Anything is possible with God. His power is beyond our understanding, and so our children can rest easy knowing "By the grace of God, I am what I am."

RIPPLES FROM THE ROCK

In "Pigskin Passion" Carlos is frustrated by the lack of a local football team. Most of his friends spend their days on the basketball courts, while Carlos dreams of yard markers and goalposts. A thoughtful conversation with his pastor gives him a new outlook and helps him find contentment in his current situation.

Pigskin Passion

The city was always a fun place to live for Carlos Hernandez. Most of his friends were in the same apartment building Carlos lived in, and there was always something exciting going on. The basketball courts out back were usually buzzing with activity, and the street out front was perfect for stickball. A good game was only a few steps away from his front door. Although Carlos loved all sports, his real passion was football. There was just something about the way that uniquely shaped ball felt in his hands that brought visions of fifty-yard touchdowns to his mind and a smile to his heart.

"Mom, when are you going to sign me up to play football?" Carlos asked one day.

"I don't know, sweetie," she replied. "I will have to look into it."

Mrs. Hernandez was a single mom working hard to provide for Carlos and his two younger sisters. She didn't want to disappoint her son, but there weren't many football leagues in the city, and the few that existed were expensive.

"Why don't you go down to the courts and shoot some hoops with Jimmy and Manny?" his mom said to him.

"Yeah, I guess I'll go see what's up," Carlos said, grabbing his football and heading for the elevator.

He jogged out of the building and over to his friends on the court. "You still carrying around that football, Carlos?" Jimmy teased. "Put it down and let's play some round ball."

"Why don't we play a little football for a change?" Carlos pleaded.

"There's no room," Manny replied.

Disappointed, Carlos dropped his football and took a shot at the hoop.

Sunday morning, as Mrs. Hernandez got her children ready for church, Carlos announced, "I want to move out of the city, Mom."

"Where's this coming from?" she replied.

"Well, there is no room around here to play football, so most of my friends just want to play basketball and stickball. I like those games, but I also want to play football. If we move someplace else where there are more parks and fields, I can play football," Carlos explained.

"I understand your frustration, honey. I would love to find a more suitable location to raise you and your sisters. Unfortunately, right now this is where my job is located. Let's take it up with God this morning at church," Mrs. Hernandez suggested.

Sitting in his usual spot up front, Carlos listened as the pastor preached about God's love.

As Carlos and his mom left church, Carlos walked up to Pastor Mike and asked, "If God loves me, how come there are no football fields near my apartment building?"

Mrs. Hernandez grabbed Carlos's arm and apologized to Pastor Mike.

"That's quite all right," the pastor replied. "It seems the young man has something on his mind." He looked at Carlos. "I will make you a deal. If you help me pick up the songbooks from the pews, I will try to explain the wonderful way God expresses His love in our lives."

"Sounds like a plan," Carlos said.

Pastor Mike and Carlos headed back into the church to start collecting the songbooks. "Okay, so give me more details about this football field you need," Pastor Mike said.

Carlos summed it up for him in one sentence: "I love football, but there's no place to play around here."

Pastor Mike agreed there were plenty of hoops in the neighborhood but not many goalposts.

"Let me ask you something, son," Pastor Mike continued. "Do you have a football?"

"Of course I do; I practically sleep with it under my pillow," Carlos replied.

"That's great!" said Pastor Mike. "Do your friends like to play football?"

"Sure, sometimes we have a catch or walk to the park for a game of two-hand touch. But they usually prefer basketball."

"So you do actually get to play football once in a while?" Pastor Mike asked.

"Well, yes, but not in an organized league or on a real field," Carlos protested.

"I hear you," Pastor Mike replied. "I was just pointing out that you do actually own a football and do get to play catch and the occasional game."

"Yeah, but it's not the same!" Carlos complained.

"Do you believe God loves you, Carlos?" Pastor Mike asked as he moved on to his next point.

"I guess. I mean, that's what you tell me every week."

"I'm glad you're listening!" Pastor Mike chuckled. "Can you name some blessings that God has given you?"

"My mom, of course," Carlos said. "My friends Jimmy and Manny."

"Those are great examples. I can name a few more: your good health, your athletic ability, a warm bed to sleep in, food on the table, clean clothes to wear—and let's not forget your football."

"I never thought about those things as blessings before," Carlos said.

They finished picking up the last few songbooks in silence.

Then Pastor Mike spoke again. "Carlos, I don't know why there aren't enough football fields in your life, but I do know that God loves you and provides what you need. Maybe you're meant to just keep practicing when and where you can until God decides to put a football team in your path, or maybe you're meant to be a basketball player and this is God's way of telling you that. The important thing is to trust God and know that He will guide you right where you need to be."

"That won't be easy, but I guess I can try," Carlos sighed as he put the last songbook away.

"It's not easy for any of us," Pastor Mike agreed.

As they locked the church doors, Pastor Mike gave Carlos some final thoughts. "When you get home, open your Bible and read Psalm 23. That is a good place to start. Then pray every day, thanking God for the blessings you do have; be sure to present your intentions and seek the grace to accept the life that He has planned for you."

There is still no football team for Carlos, but through his daily conversations with God, he is learning to live in the moment and appreciate the many blessings he does have in his life.

START THE CONVERSATION

Dear Lord, I know You are in control of all things. Help me to accept any and all results from my game or contest and to trust that You will lead me where I'm meant to be. May I truly be satisfied and content in You alone.

MORE GOOD NEWS: MATTHEW 20:1–16

God takes care of each of His children in His own special way. This story reminds us to accept the unique blessings God provides with a glad heart, content in His great love for us. We should not worry about what blessings others may receive from Him. God loves all His children and will bless in many different ways those who seek Him. It is not for us to measure or compare those blessings. Be content in God's love for you.

FIRST STEP

Help your child create a quiet space—whether indoors or out—where he or she can think and pray without distraction. Make sure the area is free from the noise of computers, television, music, and other distractions. Establish a routine before and after games to pray and reflect in this quiet place.

"HE MAKES MY FEET LIKE
THE FEET OF A DEER."

PSALM 18:33

Joy

When you obey my commandments, you remain in my love, just as I obey my Father's commandments and remain in his love. I have told you these things so that you will be filled with my joy. Yes, your joy will overflow!

—John 15:10–11 NLT

Seeing happy, well-adjusted children enjoying the sport they love brings joy to many parents. The best way to ensure our children find joy in all circumstances is to guide them to a deeper relationship with their heavenly Father. The first thing they need to do is invite God into their hearts. In John 16:24 (NAS) we are told, "Until now you have asked for nothing in My name; ask and you will receive, so that your joy may be made full." When our children place their dreams, fears, cares, and burdens in the hands of Jesus, they will be enlightened. For it is only through God's grace that joy can be experienced whether one is winning or losing. Jeremiah 15:16 (NAS) makes the case clearly: "When I found your words, I devoured them; they became my joy and the happiness of my heart."

True, lasting joy can be found only by committing to God's team and His plan. Developing a personal relationship with God through His son, Jesus, is a lifelong pursuit requiring scripture reading, prayer, reflection, and spiritual guidance. Our children should put as much—if not more—effort into building this relationship as they do into practicing their drills. Gradually, as our children learn to walk in the light of Christ, they will experience a profound sense of peace and happiness. Psalm 16:11 (NIV) proclaims, "You have made known to me the path of life; you will fill me with joy in your presence."

Winning championships or awards is extremely satisfying and uplifting. In truth, these moments are fleeting. Lasting joy can be found only through one reliable source—the Lord and Savior. By tapping and embracing the rock, our children will uncover a truth that frees them to enjoy their sport completely. Jesus assures us of this in John 8:32 (NAS): "And you will know the truth, and the truth will make you free." This treasure will be in reach when they joyfully proclaim, "By the grace of God, I am what I am."

RIPPLES FROM THE ROCK

We often hear that God listens to the prayers of His children. This goes for the cheers too! Whether the team is winning or losing, Seth's words never fail to lift the spirits of his teammates and everyone in the stands. He finds joy in the moment, and his innocent enthusiasm reminds most everyone around him about the true meaning of playing ball. You can't help but smile when you read "Cheer Leader."

Cheer Leader

As Seth bounded up the front steps of his home one afternoon, he heard a familiar sound ringing in the air.

"Mom, how come you always whistle when you're washing the floor?" he asked as he ran through the door.

"I'm not sure," she laughed. "I guess it's because I don't particularly like washing the floor, but when I whistle I feel happy."

"I don't think I understand," ten-year-old Seth replied.

"Well, I could use a break, so if you share your cookies and milk with me, I will try to explain," his mom said with a smile.

"I love our home," Seth's mom began, placing cookies on the table and sitting down. "Watching nature from the living room window is spectacular. The yard is big enough for you and your brothers to play, and for Dad's vegetable garden. I enjoy cooking and eating family meals in the oversize kitchen. But with all this good stuff comes plenty of housework."

"I take out the garbage every Tuesday and Friday night," Seth offered.

"Yes, you do," his mom acknowledged, "and that is a big help." She dunked another cookie into her glass. "Don't get me wrong. The chores are a small price to pay for the joy this house brings to our family, but I enjoy some of those tasks more than others. It's actually fun for me to wash the fluffy towels and hang them on the line outside. But getting on my hands and knees to scrub the floor is not my idea of a good time." They both finished the last of their milk as Seth's mom made her point. "That's why I whistle—to help me through the tough spots."

"I think I get it!" Seth exclaimed. "I like that you and Dad gave me my own bedroom last year, but sometimes I hear strange sounds at night that make me a little nervous. I don't want to give up my own room, so during those times I just turn on the radio and listen to music until I fall asleep."

"That's my boy," Seth's mom said. "Just remember, no matter what brings you joy in this life, there will always be times when that joy is hard to feel. Those are the times you whistle ... or listen to the radio."

Seth took his mother's lesson to heart. He loved school, except for science; so before a science test, he softly hummed a favorite tune to stay relaxed. He liked working in the yard with his dad, except for weeding; so he actually taught himself to whistle while weeding the garden. His favorite sport was baseball, except for striking out; so he made a point of cheering really hard for his teammates whenever he struck out or made an error. This helped get the focus off him and onto the next batter or another player in the field; plus, it made him feel good to support his teammates.

His new attitude did not go unnoticed on the baseball field. "C'mon! You can do it! That's the way!" His cheers echoed across the diamond and reached up to the highest bleachers.

"This boy's a true leader," remarked an assistant coach who marveled at Seth's ceaseless passion, game after game. "He brings the boys together."

Fired with the spirit, Seth breathed life into every one of his teammates. Even when he struck out, he came back to the dugout with a smile and started whooping it up for the next batter. His sheer love of baseball and the joy he felt from playing the game radiated an infectious enthusiasm.

"I believe he's the reason we turned the season around," declared a happy team parent. "He got the whole team off the bench and so pumped up they really started to believe in themselves!"

Seth could hardly believe the difference himself. He had loved baseball for as long as he could remember. But too often his joy was measured by each at bat or play in the field. It was a roller-coaster ride of great hits followed by strikeouts, or diving catches in one inning and a ball through the legs in the next.

After learning how to "whistle" through the tough spots, Seth was fully able to enjoy the game he loved, no matter what was happening on the field.

START THE CONVERSATION

Lord, I know You want the best for me. Help me to grow closer to You so that I may learn Your will for my life. Help me to trust that You are always working for good in my life—even when I may not recognize it. Help me to find joy in whatever I am doing. Amen.

MORE GOOD NEWS: ACTS 8:26–39

This story shows how the good news of Jesus Christ can change a person's life. God is always waiting patiently for us to turn our hearts and minds to Him so He can transform our lives and we can know the joy that comes from walking through life with Him.

FIRST STEP

After playing a favorite sport for a while, have your child write down how he or she feels about it, including what brings the most joy. Encourage your child to reflect on the positive emotions he or she feels when playing the sport and then write a thank-you note to God for the talents with which He has blessed your child.

Final Thoughts

Do you not know? Have you not heard? The Lord is the everlasting God, the Creator of the ends of the earth. He will not grow tired or weary, and his understanding no one can fathom. He gives strength to the weary and increases the power of the weak. Even youths grow tired and weary, and young men stumble and fall; but those who hope in the Lord will renew their strength. They will soar on wings like eagles; they will run and not grow weary, they will walk and not be faint.

—Isaiah 40:28–31 NIV

We know there are many issues in life that have higher priority than sports. Yet for so many young athletes, nothing carries more weight than the next game or contest, making youth sports a perfect entry point for developing a godly game plan for life. By using the platform of athletic competition, we can start our children on a lifetime relationship with God that will move far beyond sports into every corner of their lives. In Ephesians 2:8 (NIV), Paul tells us that God wants all His children to accept the gift of His love: "For it is by grace you have been saved, through faith-and this not from yourselves, it is the gift of God." By accepting the incredible gift of God's grace at a young age and learning to apply it to their lives, they will lay a solid foundation of faith from which they can draw much strength and direction throughout their lives.

God wants only the best for all His children. That is why He sent His son, Jesus, to bring the good news of salvation. He is saddened when a child feels helpless or alone. He is also disappointed when children forget Him during times of success. He wants an everlasting relationship with our children no matter the circumstances. In Matthew 18:12–14 (NAS), Jesus called a child to stand among the disciples while He told the parable of the lost sheep. "What do you think? If any man has a hundred sheep, and one of them has gone astray, does he not leave the ninety-nine on the mountains and go and search for the one that is straying? If it turns out that he finds it, truly I say to you, he rejoices over it more than over the ninety-nine which have not gone astray. In the same way your Father in Heaven is not willing that any of these little ones should be lost." No matter what kind of relationship you or your child have had with Him in the past, God is waiting for you now. And He will rejoice when you call His name.

Jesus says in Luke 16:10 (NAS), "He who is faithful in a very little thing is faithful also in much; and he who is unrighteous in a very little thing is unrighteous also in much." So if our children learn to trust God and give Him all the glory in the relatively minor issues of youth sports, they will be more likely to seek and receive His blessings during life's more sober moments.

The stories shared in this workbook reflect a variety of situations in which children display Christlike character in the world of youth sports. Young athletes who commit themselves to tapping the Rock and embracing the lessons put forth in this book will lay a foundation of faith and fortitude that leads to lasting treasures in sports and beyond. In Proverbs 3:5–6 (NAS) we are told, "Trust in the Lord with all your heart and do not lean on your own understanding; in all your ways acknowledge him, and he will make your paths straight." As with all good habits, the sooner our children start practicing this behavior, the more profound the results. We now realize that a complete athlete trains and develops both body and soul. Therefore, our children should continue seeking the Lord through scripture reading, prayer, church attendance, and daily conversations with Him. A life spent fulfilling God's will under the protection of His power and love is a life of peace and joy that all parents should desire for their children. And in all things, remind them of this: "By the grace of God, I am what I am."

Hidden Rock Sports, LLC, was founded to promote the role of faith in youth sports. To continue your exploration of this topic, visit HiddenRockSports.com for:

Resources to build faith and improve performance

Sports and faith in the news

Interactive blog

Inspirational products

Athletic apparel

"By the grace of God, I am what I am" (1 Corinthians 15:10).